LIFE PROFITABILITY

D1528922

LIFE PROFITABILITY

THE NEW MEASURE OF ENTREPRENEURIAL SUCCESS

ADII PIENAAR

LIONCREST
PUBLISHING

LIFE PROFITABILITY
The New Measure of Entrepreneurial Success

ISBN   978-1-5445-1852-7   *Paperback*
           978-1-5445-1851-0   *Ebook*

For my wife, Jeanne, and boys, Adii Jr. and Jamie, who have not only given me so much to live for but helped me manifest the truest me.

CONTENTS

INTRODUCTION

*My life had been building potential, potential
that would now go unrealized. I had planned
to do so much, and I had come so close.*

—Paul Kalanithi, *When Breath Becomes Air*

Neurosurgeon Paul Kalanithi had blazing ambitions and
the natural gifts to see them fulfilled. He was brilliant and
not just in one area. In 2000 he graduated from Stanford
with three degrees: a BA in human biology, and both a
BA and MA in English literature. Next came Cambridge,
where he earned an MPhil in history and philosophy of
science and medicine. He next tackled his medical degree,
graduating cum laude from the Yale School of Medicine
in 2007. During his neurological residency at Stanford,
Paul found the time to write more than twenty scientific

publications, earning recognition from his peers: he received the American Academy of Neurological Surgery's highest award for research.

In his mid-thirties, Paul's professional ambitions were coming true, but he hadn't yet fulfilled his literary dreams, nor had he yet become a father. When ambitions call, they do not whisper. They lead you forward on the path they set, and other dreams must wait until later. For Paul, later came suddenly and quickly—a lung cancer diagnosis at thirty-six. Death at thirty-seven.

Between the diagnosis and his death, Paul and his wife had a baby. She was eight months old when he died. He almost finished his book, *When Breath Becomes Air*, exploring the end of his life, but more so the meaning of his life, the life he had deferred to follow the star of his ambition. Paul's wife wrote the last chapter of his book and delivered it to the world. *When Breath Becomes Air* became a bestseller.

If you want to cry when reading, this book will bring you to that, as it did for me. And not just for the beauty and the tragedy and the triumph of Paul Kalanithi's life, but because I could see myself.

I suspect you would see yourself in it too. We are entrepreneurs, and blazing ambition lights the path before us. It doesn't, though, let us see outside and around our path, the place where the rest of our life lives. And in that way, ambition narrows our lives, our short lives.

WHEN BUSINESS CONSUMES US

There's risk in living narrowly, putting off a whole, full life for later—a risk we don't have to take. Though your lifespan might be longer than Dr. Kalanithi's, perhaps stretching out decades, if you wait to really live, the years will rush by, consumed in a blur of business and the next business challenge.

Getting a business off the ground can be all-consuming. Once it's off the ground, it has to grow, and that's consuming too. Then it must meet the challenges of profitability targets and of expansion and of employees and managing costs—it never seems to stop. In fact, the challenges attached to a successful business will never stop. Once you realize that, you also realize that having the freedom to be your own boss means not having the freedom to do what you long to do. You tell yourself you'll do it once you make another $10,000 per year or once you can catch up with demand or once you get big enough to outsource the accounting work or open that second office. Once that happens, you'll spend more time with your family or read the fat books or take that vacation.

How long have you been looking forward to that—to that future where you find the so-called work-life balance? I spent a lot of time in that purgatory before I found a better way, a way to run a thriving business that also yields what I call life profits. Had I not reshaped my business to make it life-profitable, I would have descended from purgatory to hell and lost everything that truly mattered to me—I almost did.

THE ROAD TO HELL

Like you, I started my entrepreneurial journey with good intentions. I'd always harbored ambition, and as *a* precedes *b*, so ambition precedes business. Every entrepreneur starts there, with ambition roiling the gut.

I was determined to create something of value and put it out into the world. Even in high school, I pursued business projects. In my final year, I started an alternative music record label with my friends. I continued working on that as I entered university, never allowing myself the average student experience. I sacrificed the freedom my peers had in pursuit of my business ambitions.

I met my wife, Jeanne, in university. She finds it fascinating that, even back then, I'd be sitting in our lounge, people all around me, everyone chatting, having drinks until whatever hour in the morning, and I'd be chatting too—but my laptop was always with me because I was also always working.

One of my best mates back then kept harping on about the things I was doing on the side to try to build a business. He always thought better of himself because he actually attended class and had really good grades, whereas I never attended class, so mine weren't as good.

I began asking him, "You keep saying that you're going to do this too. When are you going to start?"

And he'd always answer, "One day, one day, one day."

That was over fifteen years ago. He's a corporate employee, and he's never tried to become an entrepreneur. My conviction at the time had been right: the first step is always to start. I reasoned that it was ok to fail because I could start again until I stumbled on something. The sooner I did, the sooner I could get onto that accelerated path—the path to an elaborate, dreamy life of free time and the family I imagined for myself.

The decisions I made at university empowered and enabled me to get to where I am today. In my senior year at Stellenbosch University, I built the product that led to my first proper business, WooThemes. I quit my first postgraduation job within a matter of weeks to work at my company full-time. By then, it could support me. Within the first year or two, noticing WooThemes had become mildly successful, I suddenly realized, "Hey, this is now an actual business!" I could now title myself Successful Entrepreneur.

I'd found my place in the world. Ambition had delivered on its promise, the first part of it anyway: I had become my own boss, choosing my work and doing it my way. Financial rewards came sooner than I thought they

XIV ◇ LIFE PROFITABILITY

would. WooThemes expanded to include WooCommerce and made me my first millions. But looking back, strewn at the side of this road to success I see things I didn't even know I'd sacrificed at the time.

Turns out I couldn't enjoy the life of a student while building the business. I missed out on a part of my life— just being a student—a part I can never have again. There's no way for me to be that student again. Whether I would've liked that life or not is moot. At that stage, I thought I could do both: I could build a business and be a student at the same time. I convinced myself of that narrative. In hindsight, I realize I didn't quite believe that was true. The disappointment in all of this is that I was never truly present in the rest of my life.

FROM LIFE LOSSES TO LIFE PROFITS

So, if I wasn't present at home or with my friends or in my community, where was I? Of course, you entrepreneurs already know the answer. At all times a part of me—a large part of me—was at work, leaving a hollowed-out version of myself behind for everyone and everything else. You already guessed that because, to one degree or another, you're doing the same thing. And, as I did, maybe you've been doing it a long time. And doing it with the best intentions, even as you watch pieces of your life take damage. Of course you're willing to sacrifice yourself to the dragon.

But what about all the collateral damage? That's hard to take, isn't it?

But you don't have to take it. The missed sleep, the exercise you've forgone so long, that dinner-table stress where you're more than ready for the kids to get done so you can sprint through the dishes to get back to work, the events you've attended but missed because you were staring at your phone the entire time—all that—you don't have to live that way. Instead of bleeding life losses, your business can turn life profits. You can have space for that dinner, for every dinner, and for time with mates you've been missing for, oh, has it been a year? Workouts, quiet walks, space in your own head—a life-profitable business lets you have those again.

Life and business are not mutually exclusive. Business can—must—work for you, not the other way around. We've been conditioned to believe that being willing to sacrifice everything is the "right thing to do" and the entrepreneurial way. That's a flawed approach. Being an entrepreneur shouldn't overshadow everything. Being an entrepreneur is just one expression of life, and creating a life-profitable business can generate not only financial wealth but a rich life. The real treasure comes from having once-deferred dreams here for you *right now*—not after some unknown number of years grinding away. You are an empowered entrepreneur, living life on your own terms, just as you always wanted.

Life belongs to you. I'll be your guide.

BETWEEN THE COVERS

I'm going to teach you what life profitability means and what it looks like. I'm going to talk about achieving the space to live a whole life as a whole person. I'll show you that not only can you run a successful business that doesn't undermine the rest of your life, you can run a successful business that benefits your life. Part of how I'll do that is by sharing the strategies and tactics I employed in my latest successful business, Conversio.

You'll learn life-profitable vocabulary. With this language you'll be able to think about your business in a new way, reimagining your entrepreneurial journey and expanding your understanding of profit and loss. You'll get to define your own vision of life profits and a life-profitable business based on your own particular values. You will become the entrepreneur of your own life.

To do that, I want you to apply all the entrepreneurial talents and strengths you use in business to your life. This is *your* dream life to build, though, not someone else's. Because of this, I cannot tell you the specific steps to live *your* profitability. This is not a how-to book. It is a tool for evaluating your life's underfed parts and then moving toward fullness by learning from my hard-won lessons.

This being the case, you won't find formulas that would substitute my way of doing things for your own. You'll forge your own path in true entrepreneurial fashion, adding life-profitable dimensions to your particular business, making your particular adjustments to grow life profits while eliminating life losses. I'll provide some strategies and tactics to move you toward that.

And just as you wouldn't stop monitoring your business's financial health, you cannot expect to read the last page of this book, close the cover, and think you're set. Your signature must be on a pact you reach with yourself to live right now and start measuring your business success by its life profits from now on.

Getting the Most from This Book

Though I'd like you to read this book in order instead of jumping around, being an entrepreneur, I know that some of you are already thinking, I'll do it my own way, thanks. And if you're one of those people who is not only an entrepreneur but one of those mavericks who reads book endings—even fiction book endings—before reading the beginnings, I know I have little chance of convincing you to stay the course with me.

All right. But some concepts must lead the way if you're to actually put this into practice. Chapter 2 explains life profitability, while Chapter 3 explains the starting point of creating life profitability—yourself, not your business.

Some of you are skimmers too, especially if your business is decidedly life-unprofitable, leaving you little time for anything else. Skimming will give you a grounding, and that's a start. You might even be able to make some small adjustments, freeing up space to reread the book to take on bigger changes.

But if you truly want to get the most from your time investment the first time around, read the book from start to finish and reflect. You'll have the chance to do that at the end of every chapter, where you'll find a quote to think about, as well as reflection prompts. These reflections will serve as your travel log, as it were, so ideally, write down your thoughts. You'll refer back to them in the final chapters of the book as you begin finding opportunities to plan how you'll build life profits.

If recording thoughts by writing doesn't appeal, consider audio recordings. Another alternative—one I use myself—is to highlight ideas that resonate and comment on them. It's a way to do a bite-sized reflection in real time as you read. When I highlight and now and again stop to take notes on my phone, at least, it's like leaving little breadcrumbs for myself. These breadcrumbs can add up to a whole loaf by the time you get to the book's end. Do give time to the prompts, even if it's a quick look and reaction. Starting in Chapter 9, you'll be using your own thoughts to build up your business's capacity to grow its life profits.

WHY LISTEN TO ADII?

Just like you, I started my entrepreneurial journey with ideas and expectations about the path I'd travel and what I'd have to do to reach my desired destination. Long hours, intense focus, living the business above all else—this was the atmosphere around my business calling, and I was willing to breathe it in. I even outfitted myself to weather this climate, adopting certain "must-have" entrepreneurial accoutrements of the time—for instance, a Herman Miller Aeron chair (which proved a great investment). I wanted to give myself what I thought was every chance of success. I could see that success in the someday of my future, so I thought the faster I went at it, the harder I did it, the more endurance and grit and determination I exercised, the sooner I'd get there.

I loved it, but I also felt all the hardship, misery, and eventual burnout common to entrepreneurs. The sprinting and slogging depleted me. I willingly stuck with it because I thought it was the price entrepreneurs had to pay. I stuck with it even when this worry crept in, a sense that my business and life itself were at odds with one another in a sort of war, me in the no-man's-land between them. I just thought I had to get through it: after this phase would come enough success. Enough success would justify any injuries. Enough success would mean enough reward—reward enough to make me and my life whole, enough to make it all worth it.

Enough success came. Business took off in all the standard ways that herald it: sales, profits, clients, financial wealth. But it wasn't reward enough. The success didn't make me whole. I was an unhappy multimillionaire. And I was about to get even unhappier.

All the money in the world can't patch up the holes in your life, the holes you bore out by following the typical entrepreneurial path. But I didn't know any other way. I took a sabbatical, but within six months had another idea that set my entrepreneurial brain on fire. My wife, Jeanne, feigned surprise, but she knew who I was. I was off to the races again.

And again came the same sense of depletion, of life being hollowed out, only worse this time. And that sense of existential worry that the business and life itself were at odds? That turned into a near certainty. My business and my life—marriage, children, everything personal—they were mutually exclusive. I was ready to admit defeat. I just could not fulfill the duties of my personal life at the same time as I built another business that would set my family up forever.

I am a family man. It is one of my deepest core values, necessary to my best life. And I am an entrepreneur. I could not change myself. But I could change *how* I lived out being an entrepreneur. Before I resigned from my family, before I threw it all away, I stopped and looked around, got my bearings, sought new ways of thinking and living.

And I began reining in the dragon that had become my business. I didn't do a 180, starving it out. I just began feeding it less of me and less of my life, redistributing, reimagining, reinventing my methods of doing business. I doubled down on my best self. I began challenging the unquestioned assumptions we all have about what an entrepreneur is and does. I began demanding that my business benefit my life—right now, not later. I tested different approaches and practices, refining them and adjusting them to resurrect my life and benefit the lives of my employees and my greater community. I began accumulating a new vocabulary to check myself and check my business, a business that successfully yielded life profits. A business that got out of the red as far as life profitability was concerned.

My life-profitable business made my life rich and full well before I ended up selling it, also for millions. But that wasn't the measure of my success. My happiness; the happiness of my family; my sense of wholeness, of living from the seat of my own governance, centered and aligned with who I am—those signaled my success. I was living the dream—my dream.

I had found the ways to build a financially robust business that also helped build a robust life for me and my employees. I want that for you too. Life and business are not mutually exclusive. In fact, your business can serve your life right here, right now. You do not have to defer your life and dreams.

Let's begin making your life profitable.

CHAPTER ONE

CHALLENGING THE ENTREPRENEURIAL ARCHETYPE

The cost of a thing is the amount of what I will
call life which is required to be exchanged
for it, immediately or in the long run.
—Henry David Thoreau, *Walden*

We entrepreneurs all start with a definite list of improvements for a better life. Maybe more freedom is the upgrade you want, freedom to do what you want, when you want to do it. Maybe life improves when you never again have to think, *I don't want to work overtime for this soul-sucking boss. I want to go home to my family.* Or maybe your "My Better Life" list just has one thing: "Afford a Ferrari." It doesn't matter what it is. What matters is that it feeds your ambition to change something in your life for the better, and typically not just for you but for those around you.

Ambition is a powerful friend, courageous too, pushing you to break with the status quo and start the business. When ambition promised that a business could make life better, you believed it. That's why you agreed to clothe yourself in the entrepreneur label, even though it meant breaking from safe acceptability. Entrepreneur is a label designing bespoke lives to whatever specifications you want. Freedom, owning your own time, owning the fruits of your labor—the Ferrari!—those are the deliverables. They're why you do it—work the eighty hours, come late to your own birthday party, forget to eat. The ultimate goal and the true driver of ambition is to change some part of your life. You're doing it all for the promised rewards that will come someday to transform your life for the better.

But those rewards come with a cost.

THE REAL COST OF DOING BUSINESS

Entrepreneurs think of cost in a straightforward, linear way of input-output. For instance, you put in money, you get out employee labor. Labor means a product or service, which, in turn, gets traded for money coming in. Or you pay for a marketing campaign and the beneficial result is new paying customers.

We also understand that the money we have right now is finite, so spending it on something means not spending it on something else. We know that about time too. If I assign Project A to my employees, they can't spend that same time on Project B. Time is a precious resource. We know that at such a gut level that we say "time is money."

Time is also life, but life is not money. You can't invest life and get it back later. It's not like money, where you can trade it for marketing and then see it boomerang back, maybe even with extra money tagging along. Your life is the most important cost of doing business.

Your lifetime only has so much time, and it only moves in one direction. There's a starting point, an ending point, and in between there's time, our constant companion, time that is always in the process of running out. Our heart provides the beat as we march down our timeline, wisely or foolishly—it's all the same. Where you spend time and energy, you spend your life. This moment in your timeline is labeled Entrepreneurial Era in big, bold letters to show its importance. How long have you been living there? How much of your life has this era already drained?

What a gamble we entrepreneurs take. After all, our days are numbered. And so are the days of our loved ones.

GAMBLING WITH OUR LIVES

Entrepreneurs trade certain freedoms for the pursuit of entrepreneurial liberty. And we must: starting a business demands so much from us that we're forced to forsake other freedoms. The archetypical entrepreneurial journey narrative tends to glorify this sacrifice to business first and foremost, dominating our every waking hour. It takes up a lot of room in our psyche, a mass of plans and worry and coordination and juggling, all of this under pressure. It's so dense and large that it has its own gravity. Even when we try to leave it behind, take a break, take a holiday, it pulls at us.

No matter how much we enjoy the attraction, we also sense that it's not right. We feel guilty as we cheat on our lives. Then the day comes when you realize that going back to your life to spend time on friends or hobbies or exercise or, well, anything else, feels like you're cheating on your business. Our business passion has become an obsession we suffer. And that's fitting: the Latin root for the word *passion* means suffering.

There's an element in all of this that speaks to toxic masculinity. For centuries, rich white men have run this whole construct of entrepreneurship and business. The archetype following along tells entrepreneurs you have to be a "man," and "man" is supposed to mean a certain something shot through with socialized paternalism and maleness.

Which makes femaleness an opposite to entrepreneurialism. As an antonym to male, female—excuse the expression—is the odd man out. Even if women manage to somehow embody all the so-called masculine traits the archetype requires, they do not have the actual body that qualifies. Meanwhile, for both men and women, the archetype reinforces pain as power, pain as legitimacy. Pain is supposed to be a good sign. The more the better.

The entrepreneurial archetype tells us we're "supposed" to suffer and sacrifice, all the while devoted and dedicated, enduring the costs—the collateral damage—of trying to build a business. It assumes that following a life sequence of business first, life later will give us the best chance of success. If we want the fame, status, and material wealth, the security of equity and ownership in this future we are trying to create—to get ahead instead of just drawing a salary by swapping time for it—we must go all in, in every way.

The simple hypothesis is that people working sixty- or eighty-hour weeks can outwork their competitors, assuming you're not doing the completely wrong things. Then, over time, you can probably gain some kind of competitive advantage. That incentivizes you to make all these sacrifices in life and to reinvest the dividends of those sacrifices—time, energy, attention—back into the business for the possible commercial edge. It seems like a sound gamble.

But, of course, it is still a gamble, and it's not just money you're wagering. Just how much are you willing to lose? You're assuming success on the other side, but failure rates are high. You're betting your life, possibly a lifetime, that you will "win."

Most entrepreneurs, probably most people in the West, think of a successful business as one that can look forward to infinite growth into an infinite future. Because we seldom challenge that notion, entrepreneurs often develop a "growth at all costs for as long as it takes" mindset. But we seldom take inventory and count up the costs to our lives, even though we feel the subtraction. What are you feeding your business, that growing dragon with the insatiable appetite? How expensive are these feedings, and how long will you have to bear these costs?

Businesses being built as fast as possible to grow according to expectations of infinity can yield only marginal happiness to the ever-laboring entrepreneurs behind them. The open-ended timeframe of the venture alone may mean not only life deferred but life missed altogether—a business gobbling up your numbered days for a success that never comes. You might tell yourself you'll quit at some artificial milestone, you'll just get off the hamster wheel when there's x more money, x more material, x more property, x more success.

Two problems with that. First, it's hard to predict when you'll actually achieve x more anything. Are you supposed to put your life on hold until then? Second, you're an entrepreneur. Maybe you will hold yourself to your promise, but probably not. Maybe you're more like me, unable to even last through the break I'd planned for myself after selling my share of WooThemes. Ambition strikes and you're back at it again. Regardless of the success we achieve, ambition dictates that there's more to be achieved. An arbitrary stopping point is unlikely to hold you back. Meanwhile, you're suffering, and likely so are those around you.

When you add up all the life costs of the business to you and your family, the disappointments, absences, missed experiences, stress, sleep deprivation—all the quality and quantity of life time—you'll probably find your business is running a net life loss even if it is turning a financial profit. The gains cannot offset the loss. The life sequence plan of business first, life later isn't so much a plan as a scheme. It makes little sense to sacrifice so much of your life now in the hope that someday, some way, it will reincarnate into a better, though shortened, life later. Even my rapid business success, with all its financial gain, didn't justify use of that life-sequence model. Doing it that way, my business success was bankrupting the rest of my life.

But it was "expected of me," a test of my entrepreneurial mettle.

THE NON-SOLUTION OF
WORK-LIFE BALANCE

I'm not suggesting the solution is to get rid of a business running at a life loss, just the assumptions you've made about how you have to go about running it. I'm sure many of you, experiencing the unsustainability of prioritizing business over actual living, have tried to go about it in a different way already, aiming for the so-called work-life balance. Work-life boundaries can't make your business life-profitable either, though. It's a flawed approach, a binary choice that relies on compartmentalizing. In other words, to practice it, you must divide yourself and store these pieces in silos with as little cross contamination as possible. Those of you who have tried this know it's impossible.

It may be easier to do if you're working for someone else, knowing that "this job is just my nine-to-five gig, and at least on a Friday when I close my office door for the last time this week, I will not think about work again until maybe Sunday evening." But most entrepreneurs struggle to disconnect from work. You never stop thinking about it, whether it's out of fear of losing ground or from an obsession about gaining more. You never, ever have that freedom again of just living life. Business and your entrepreneurial journey are always an undercurrent, omnipresent. And our technology makes the struggle to disconnect even harder. Work is in our pockets; we feel the weight of it there, the pull of it with every notification. In my WooThemes days, I worked from 7 a.m. to about 7 p.m., a twelve-hour day. I felt I had to be in the office first to lead by example. And I had to leave last, for the same reason. Then, as life became thornier due to all the sacrifices and mounting collateral damage, those twelve-hour days became an escape from the rest of my life.

But, of course, I was not productive during all that work time. People working sixty- or eighty-hour weeks aren't productive. I think all the research and science these days shows that not even Superman can do that amount of proper, efficient, productive knowledge work for that amount of time. The ratio of efficiency and productivity per hour greatly diminishes, which, in terms of life profitability, meant that I could've better spent this time elsewhere, even if it just meant rejuvenating and bringing a fresh mind to the same work challenges the next day. I could have gone for a run or spent time with my family, but I didn't know to do that then. I didn't consider those alternatives or a mindset change about how I could be working and should be working.

My schedule did give me an evening cutoff point where I could seesaw to the life side of the work-life balance. But who was I bringing home? Even supposing I could have disconnected my work brain, I'd left most of my energy and ability to focus at work. I could only feed my life the leftovers of myself, sometimes mere crumbs of myself. In this way, work-life balance is just the work first, life later sequence in another guise, practiced on a daily scale. When we try to make living and working equal and mutually exclusive, we make them enemies of each other, locked in a constant struggle.

As entrepreneurs, we shouldn't be caught in a two-dimensional construct of either work to live or live to work. We've got to think more three-dimensionally. Work is just one node of your life, a significant one to be sure, but there are many significant nodes—children, perhaps, a spouse, your parents. There's your physical and mental health. Your craving for meaning. You must decide where your life energy ought to flow, how much of it and when, moving fluidly throughout your life's nodes, of which your business is just one. Life itself, however, is the field underlying everything; it's the context within which your business operates. Not the other way around.

REJECTING THE ENTREPRENEURIAL ARCHETYPE

It's time for you to stop running your life according to some societal script of what an entrepreneur looks and acts like. If you don't know where to start or feel a sense of uncertainty here, you're in the perfect place to reenvision your own entrepreneurial journey and write its rules and norms. You are, after all, an entrepreneur, and part of being a successful entrepreneur is navigating uncertainties, finding answers for questions, and finding solutions for problems. In this book, you're going to become the entrepreneur of your life.

First, though, you have to take a leap of faith that it is possible to *not* follow the entrepreneurial template and still achieve a thriving business. I did it. You can too. Decide to experiment with new ways of doing business and to commit to a life lived now. To be the entrepreneur of your life, you will have to tolerate risk and uncertainty, and the roller-coaster experience of immense highs and immense lows, just as you did when you started up your business. But all of these experiences will have an enriching effect as you create a life-profitable business. They will add value to your life instead of devaluing it. It's important to find fulfillment in every step of the journey. That gives you a higher chance of success in terms of life profitability. None of us can ensure business success. Economies collapse and take companies down; a new invention can render whole industries irrelevant or redundant; a plague can cut a swath through your workforce, grinding your business to a halt. Your life profits cannot be taken from you, though.

You may also have to confront imposter syndrome, a commonplace complaint amongst entrepreneurs. You may already struggle with it, feeling you haven't actually earned the success you have now. Despite all you've done—all you've given—to get where you are, imposter syndrome may tell you that blood, sweat, and tears don't count to earn you a spot at the table. It will recall all the times you didn't really know what you were doing, how you were—still are—always a learner and never an expert. You're no Branson or Jobs. And now I'm asking you to refuse to play the part assigned to you, the archetypal entrepreneur who hustles to the point of health problems, bounces between tasks like two squirrels playing Ping-Pong, and pushes through obstacles via single-minded focus, leaving a debris field in your wake.

Imposter syndrome might ask you, "Are you really an entrepreneur if you don't play this part?" Imposter syndrome wants you to conform to the entrepreneurial archetype.

You'll have to remind it that conformity and initiative don't naturally sit together. Initiative likes innovation better. And conformity never stands up and declares, "Right. Well, I'm going to change the status quo. I'm going to create something of value here. I'm starting a business."

But an entrepreneur does. We entrepreneurs believe that you can change the status quo through a combination of ambition, clever ideas, and hard work. If we stubbornly stick to that formula, we will eventually run through the brick wall that separates success and failure. It's the typical entrepreneurial formula.

But being stubborn is not a great feeling. It's rigid and inflexible, and running through a brick wall can't be pleasant either. It leaves people feeling like failures as they discover *My head is bloodied. I can't do this anymore.*

But, of course, they're not failures. They're people who recognize an unsustainable future but don't know how to save the situation.

Much of the entrepreneurial success story is very black and white: are you making money or are you losing money? There's no perspective there, no way to measure for something else where you can say, "Yes, perhaps I failed for the narrow definition of success, but for the last five years, I actually built a pretty great life with this business." Running a business has benefits beyond a narrow definition of success. Your investment is more than money, and it pays out more than money too—especially if you intend it to.

Now that you understand that society has given us a sort of one-script-fits-all for your business journey and that your definition of success doesn't have to be so narrow, you can decide to write your own business adventure. You can decide for yourself what success looks like and aim for more than just business riches but life riches as well. You can also learn to more fully count business costs by expanding your expenses to include the life riches your business has embezzled from you.

Recall what Henry David Thoreau said: "The cost of a thing"—your business—"is the amount of what I will call life which is required to be exchanged for it, immediately or in the long run." How much of your life are you spending on it now? What are the consequences you'll pay later? If you were gone tomorrow, would your legacy of intense investment into your business sit well with you? Would it sit well in the hearts of your loved ones? Would they have enough good memories to carry them through the rest of their lives? Would friends and acquaintances recall you narrowly, describing you as "very devoted to business" and "hardworking and driven" and "first in, last to go"? There's a sad meagerness in that final, settled version of you, a verdict, really, of you the entrepreneur.

You can create your own entrepreneurial model. It's time to stop racking up life losses. Instead, you must learn how to make your business start turning life profits alongside financial profits. Let's get you back to your ultimate goal: having the room for more freedom and the means to live a whole and rich life. In the next chapter we'll explore life profitability, a new way of thinking about profit and gain.

REFLECTION

"It is not the man who has too little who is poor, but the one who hankers after more."

—Seneca

What is your idea of a successful entrepreneur, and how has pursuing that made you poorer in life riches?

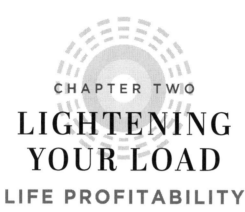

CHAPTER TWO

LIGHTENING YOUR LOAD

LIFE PROFITABILITY EXPLAINED

*In the measurement world, you set a goal
and strive for it. In the universe of possibility,
you set the context and let life unfold.*
—Benjamin Zander, *The Art of Possibility:
Transforming Professional and Personal Life*

L ike most everyone else in the West, we entrepreneurs have an unhealthy relationship with measurement. In the West, we often leave no room between measurement and passing judgment. Think of any popular measurement—height, weight, income, net worth—you'll find that all of us have a standard "ideal" that has been fed to us and against which we give or do not give a seal of approval. This being the case, we entrepreneurs are well aware that everyone we know will judge us according to "success" standards.

We tend to measure everything in business. We do so not only because we need information with which to make decisions and set goals, but because we want a snapshot on whether or not we "measure up." Measure up to what? Mostly others and the unsustainable and merciless expectations set by the entrepreneurial archetype.

Are the numbers moving in the right direction? How do they compare with my competition? Are we moving quickly enough? How productive are we? Can we wring out any more efficiency? How much of a footprint do we have on social media? How many people are showing love by sharing?

When such questions are tinged, maybe soaked, with the fear and worry of not measuring up, we begin to give the measuring of things our rapt and undivided attention. And against the waking nightmare of falling short, of not properly measuring up, we labor, and we labor hard, and we start to feel that we live or die according to measurements. From objective data bits that help us make informed decisions, measurement rises to the role of judge. We fear the judgment, and when it goes our way, we welcome it as proof—a vindication of the risks we took and the sacrifices we made—and we want it to continue.

In the shadows of that are feelings of life and death, the suffering our egos will undergo if the numbers paint a lackluster or even terrible picture of our business, which in our minds is a direct reflection of self. When we let the business embody us, we must have numbers that vouch for us, numbers that tell us and others that we are, indeed, a bona fide entrepreneur and, therefore, for that measurement snapshot at least, worthy.

But the measurement focus is a trap in several different ways. For one thing, the entrepreneurial canon dictates that the numbers should always increase. That creates a situation that can turn otherwise "good" metrics like growth into disappointment when growth is less than the quarter before.

Of course, we invest all the resources we can into all the things that will move those kingmaker, king-slayer measurements in a direction that better favors us. Once measurement takes on its own life, it demands a certain fealty, commanding not just intellectual attention, but emotional attention as well. Measurement will tell you if you are living or if you are dying. We typically don't stop to wonder, to really consider how important these measurements are in the larger context of our lives. And we don't stop to consider, in the larger context of our lives, whether we're even measuring the right things.

The measurement world is indifferent to things such as inspiration, deviation, or improvisational growth. It doesn't care about lessons learned that pay later dividends, unearthed opportunities that can lead to something even better, and it doesn't care about life profits. The measurement world is not a place for the organic, for riotous life vining and fruiting according to circumstances and clever opportunism, the place of assertive success. Measurement is a reductionist world that pronounces death, life, or being on the verge of one of those. Measurement has a place, an important and useful place, but it should not be the center of your universe.

A UNIVERSE OF POSSIBILITY

The universe is not reductionist. Nor is it limited, unlike measurement, which, by definition, is. After all, you can only measure quantity, and only the quantity of what you think to measure. Measurement is really only feedback on how close you are to a goal or milestone, regardless of other mitigating considerations. And then, looking at the differential between the measurement and the target, you judge your efforts and past plans.

If the universe is not strict, judgmental, and mechanistic, what is it?

Possibility. The context you set is the field of possibility where you plant the seeds of life and nourish their growth and harvests. What is your universe of possibility? What is your context, the field where life will grow?

You will find it where quality of life is welcomed and intended, where the seeds you plant yield meaningful experiences, wisdom, challenges, joy, and discovery. Lived meaning emboldens and encourages us; it nourishes and comforts instead of sapping us.

What if your life was set in the universe of possibilities and given a context of meaning and fulfillment right now? Not later, after you've spent your life in the reduced circumstance of a business driven by measurements commanding your actions.

Life is supposed to be whole and wholesome, worthy of your humanity and that of those you love. Your life is naturally holistic and synthesized, realizing all of yourself and the dreams that fuel your ambitions. Just like your body cannot be understood by referencing only a leg or a toe, your life cannot be understood only as a function of your business. The most meaningful experiences you will ever have are mostly not with work and not with colleagues. If you stop filtering all your life through your business, you have the chance for a purer life. And if you start filtering your business through life, you have the chance to make it add to your life instead of taking from it.

This is important because, even if your business is wildly successful, money is not going to achieve your life's goals. Just measuring the monetary success and saying, "Hey, my bank funds are growing significantly every single month!" is a very limited way of trying to ascertain where you are in your life. Taking a life-first approach not only sets the proper context in your universe of possibility; it opens your eyes to new ways of measuring success.

Life first means, for instance, that when you run a marathon, yes, you want to run at a certain time for a certain distance. You have to measure that. But having the discipline of running every single day, finding that it centers you and that you feel great afterward—you do great work afterward—that's much, much harder to measure. And those kind of measurement-resistant feelings and experiences we enjoy as we live—those are what we're going for. You need time for them, space for them, and your business must yield to them.

You don't have to give up your ambition. You don't have to give up your entrepreneurial journey. You just need to expand your ambition to include your life lived now. You just need to tweak the itinerary for your journey so that it goes beyond being yoked to your business, traveling head down, and missing all the enjoyable sights. You want your life to profit by your efforts. By making your business yield to life, your business can yield life profits. It will do this by the way you ask it to perform going forward and by judging its performance not only by traditional measurements but also by how it has helped you live.

LIFE PROFITS

In a nutshell, realizing life profits means more lived abundance for every person the business touches. This is the vision, the mission, the strategy, and its outcome. A richer, more colorful life that is so much wider and deeper than a business will look different to every entrepreneur since it's based on you and what you value. The burdens you bear for your business often sacrifice those valued things—things that make life worth living. Those burdens are business costs to your life. By challenging the traditional paradigm of success and the obligation you feel to adopt it, you lighten the burden. Jettisoning those and writing your own definition of success means reconsidering business profits and the pursuit of more in the context of what life treasures you have been giving up.

Making more space for your life when you are used to feeling obligated to give your business your all might feel scary and daunting. But you're not going to make a drastic change to the way things are right now. It's important not to do a 180-degree turn here, but instead begin growing life profits by shifting the way you do things in incremental bits. Within business there are rules and ethics that must be upheld. But you can play the game in a changed way by differently orienting yourself to it.

Orienting toward a meaningful life as the context in which your business operates reconnects your business with your humanness. It allows for an interplay between work and life. For instance, you take that thirty-minute coffee meetup that you've been putting off for so long. Your business dragon will likely speak to you in a discouraging way, saying things like "Oh, I don't really want to see this person. This is probably not going to be great. I could do so much more here." But running a life-profitable business means you go ahead and take that meetup anyway.

And if that meeting starts turning into an interesting, rewarding two-, three-, four-, even five-hour thing where you start canceling other business duties where you are probably being measured—where you're needed to perform some task or work on some deliverable or communicable outcome—you let life win. You must be open to that, daring to do such a thing because life rewards us with unexpected dividends when we engage with it. You don't know where you're going to find meaning, and you don't know how far that interaction might ripple. It could end up being one of the highlights of the week. When you find yourself in that enjoyable, promising moment, you let meaning unfold. Such things are much more significant, much more meaningful in aggregate than anything you can do at work during that time.

A happy entrepreneur who has a meaningful life is probably also doing their best work more consistently and doing it in a more sustainable way. Making your business life-profitable by making small shifts creates a cycle where life profits end up flowing back into the business through better engagement. When people feel both a sense of meaning and productive, they do meaningful things at work. Work that is ultimately profitable helps the business achieve the business goals but also creates a certain life-supportive environment in which you do that.

There are various ways to create that supportive environment, ways that may allow you to work seven hours a day instead of eight, nine, or ten hours a day. That, in turn, leads to more life profits and better engagement when at work. When you work seven hours a day for 90 percent of your workdays in a year, you don't go home feeling so lethargic and carrying all that baggage about what happened at work. You're not still fighting in your head with this customer, or that supplier, or this team member. Your business won't subtract from the life space that is supposed to be dedicated to your most meaningful pursuits. And the time you've given back to your life can be spent in activities that feed your heart, body, mind, and soul. Imagine how much better you will show up in your life with this shift. Think of the better you who will arrive at work the next day.

The interplay between business and life, and life and business is always present, no matter how we try to separate them. If I walk out of my home office and face another stressful situation—say, there is a sudden blackout or the kids are being difficult or my wife and I have an unresolved disagreement—work stress won't just evaporate to make room. Stressful things linger and fuel each other. And then, tomorrow will come, and I will bring the day before to work, where I face more stress, and then I bring it home again. It becomes a vicious cycle.

When you relieve heaviness in favor of lightness, and then take an intentionally more wholesome approach to that interplay between work and life, that's where you can find opportunity for life profitability. Instead of a vicious cycle, you create a life profit cycle that lets you bring a better self into bettering your business. I go for a run during lunch to release some of the bottled-up work stress. I purposely take evening time relaxing with my family, knowing I'll be more peaceful come work. I put my phone out of reach of my bed. I do not sleep with the business dragon. It is not within biting distance. My bed is where I sleep in peace.

No entrepreneur builds a business to *not* be profitable in a financial sense, especially if they have people who work for them. Having spoken to many entrepreneurs, having a team is one of the factors that keeps them working really hard. Many business owners will take pay cuts themselves so that they can afford payroll for their team, first and foremost. But the responsibility toward employees can't be the only factor in how we entrepreneurs choose how much and in which ways we work.

You can't just go to work to figure out how to build a business that pays everyone's paychecks. Eventually, those kinds of motivations just fizzle out in the heat of burnout. It's that cycle again: you take the bad stuff from work into life, feeling burnt out and getting less and less recovery from life and then infuse a subpar version of yourself back into work. Instead of blocking life out in favor of your business responsibilities, begin looking at yourself and your life holistically. Prioritize what you value to home in on what gives your life meaning and nourishment, those things that accumulate well-rounded wealth in terms of wholeness. With this new way of seeing and thinking, you will find opportunities on your entrepreneurial journey to feed your deeper needs.

LIFE SETS THE TABLE; BUSINESS PROVIDES THE FOOD

At this point you may be wondering what business life profitability looks like in the real world. Glad you asked! I have wonderful memories of life profitability in action, ways that my business created space for my life to flourish—and not just mine, but the lives of people I love. There is that time that I got invited to speak at a software conference in Boston in 2011. My wife, Jeanne, accompanied me there. It was her first time in Boston. And it was around our second wedding anniversary. I managed to surprise her by flying us out to California to see...a Justin Bieber concert because she was totally into Justin Bieber at the time.

Yes, I flew all the way from Cape Town, South Africa, to America, and then all the way to the West Coast to see a Justin Bieber concert with a bunch of screaming teenage girls.

I love my wife.

More recently, I was paid to be at a conference in Bali. It was a great opportunity to have a family trip. Instead of paying travel expenses for all of us, I only had to pay for my wife and two children. That in itself is already a benefit, but then having the whole family there, seeing me in my actual state of happiness on that stage, sharing it with me—those are magical moments that a life-profitable approach to business can create.

And for me, on a regular basis, such meaningful moments are even simpler. One of the best parts of my day, one that sadly came to an end because my youngest son, Jamie, changed schools, was our after-school reunion. For the last couple years, he went to a little preschool, literally a kilometer away from us. He would come home at one o'clock, and the first thing he would do was run into my office and jump onto my lap. And then we would have ten- or fifteen-minute argy-bargy, and then follow it up with just a chat about his day.

Family, as I told you previously, is one of my core values. It is meaningful enough to dictate action like a compass I can consult to keep me on course in life. I work from home, and to have that interaction with Jamie in the midst of my workday, even if some days it can only be five minutes, reinforces the understanding that business serves life, and that life is paramount, the point of the whole endeavor.

Life first means living as close to your nature as possible instead of trying to fit yourself into an external construct. Doing that lets you tap your strengths and bring them into the world. Instead of friction, there is flow.

RECONSIDER THE CONCEPTS OF TIME, MONEY, AND HAPPINESS

Reading that a successful life-profitable business puts life first might cause you some anxiety or at least tension, even if you know you can't go on the way you have been. We all want our businesses to be successful in the measurement world, where we can point to numbers—healthy profits, a growing customer base, top ratings, and the like. This is where you need to weigh the life costs of doing business and reflect on how much is enough, especially if it's costing you, your family, and your employees a greater, richer life. The business dragon is insatiable. It's up to you to set limits on how much you feed it, redistributing time, attention, and energy to your larger life in the universe of possibility. But first, let's reconsider how we think of time, money, and happiness.

Time

Steve Jobs said, "My favorite things in life don't cost any money. It's really clear that the most precious resource we all have is time." We would probably all agree with Jobs here. Time is precious because it provides the space for us to enjoy our favorite things, the things that create meaning and memories. For Jobs, those favorite things weren't material. Your favorite things probably don't cost anything either. Time with family, watching the sunrise or sunset, a good night's sleep with some great dreams—none of those cost money.

Right now, you may be wondering, *But how do I devote time to life outside work?* So far, you've probably "bought back" time with takeout and hiring someone else to do various jobs. But you've likely sunk that time back into your business instead of your life because you need to keep producing the money to buy that time. So, fundamentally, you've not changed the way this system works. As soon as you stop working, you suddenly lose the time as well. This keeps business at the center of things, the context for everything else. So, first, you must remember that the context for your business is you and not the other way around.

Remember, once you start working on that hamster wheel and it gets to spinning, it's very hard to get off. The faster it spins, the harder it is to apply force in the opposite direction, which is why many people find themselves, years down the line, waking up from this semicomatose state thinking, *Shit, I obviously got to this point in a very specific and certain way, but I feel lost. I thought that I was making all these decisions, but I was actually allowing this mainstream narrative of how to spend my time just play out and impose itself on my life. And where am I? I never really stopped to find myself relative to my path. I'm lost to myself.*

A sad feature of this is that in the world of measurement, you can measure the revolutions of that hamster wheel. You can measure all the energy you spent on the hamster wheel. You can measure all sorts of things on the hamster wheel, including the time spent there. But your natural life hasn't expanded and deepened. You've aged, which you could measure too, but in terms of happiness and meaningfulness, the hamster wheel claimed your life. All the accumulated measures turn out to run long but weigh nothing because they're actually spent things.

One of the ways this happens is that we have an unquestioned binary and simplistic approach to time: there's work time and there's life time, and we believe that we must work harder and longer for success. By segregating time this way, we shrink life and even exclude it. Again, the world of measurement tends toward one focus. One focus makes us default into a strategy of exclusion.

Instead of thinking of work time as the time to exclude all else, we must start to find overlap with our lives, letting there be an interplay between them. And we must use time in a way that aligns with and supports our nature.

For instance, if it's been a harder week, I tend to have slower Fridays, even if I'm not as productive. And sometimes, that's how my Friday mornings start: me largely unproductive, dabbling through my work. And then, come five or six o'clock, I find energy to do something really productive and work. I don't try to force myself into a time straitjacket. I flow as myself naturally, and in that way, I am happier and do better work. I accomplish more in the productive times, and during the less productive times, I may be coasting but am still moving ahead, conserving and building energy.

I might do some work on the weekends when the house is quiet. I decide intentionally that I actually want to do work. It's not that I feel the dragon breathing down my neck. It's my choice. This is about adopting a whole-life perspective, looking at the circumstances, and recognizing what that actually means for you in that moment. Time is a form of space, and space always has a life context, the way the rooms in your house provide a context for the activities that ought to go on in them. Don't default to work with every spare moment. Instead, look at time as a contextual space and ask yourself what's appropriate for that time setting.

Money

In our Western world, we glorify the pursuit of wealth and its endless accumulation. We glorify money so much so that we measure our self-worth by our net worth too often and measure ourselves against others by what they own. This puts us in an escalating "arms race" for material goods as we try to keep up with the Joneses. When someone else has more, we believe we should be able to have as much or more as well, and we fall into that measurement world focus trap that keeps us yoked to our businesses.

Money makes us spend a lot of time in the measurement world counting it up and exchanging set amounts of our time for it. We do this because we think that money lets us purchase happiness and that more money lets us purchase more happiness. It's not that simple. Argentinian writer-philosopher José Narosky said, "Whoever exchanges happiness for money can't exchange money for happiness."

Is there happiness in keeping up with the Joneses when you never find peace and an end to the material goods arms race? Seeing someone in a less expensive car than yours and fleetingly feeling proud of your own—that's not happiness either. And you definitely won't find happiness at the grander home of an acquaintance where you feel like an underperformer who ought to be earning more.

When we exchange time for money to engorge our bank accounts, we surrender our universe of possibility. We give ourselves over, losing the chance to use time in *meaningful* ways that bring us happiness. Essentially, then, we trade happiness for money. If we do that over the course of a lifetime, we have given up a lifetime of happiness.

Money is an efficient middleman that lets us exchange the product of our labors with that of another's. It lets us quickly get what we need with one trade instead of a chain of them. That's all money is—an efficient middleman. After we trade it to meet our needs, the rest of our spending is on wants at best, covetousness at worst. Certainly, having nice things can feel great. Spending money for experiences can feel great as well, and can be enriching. But spending happiness to live in the measurement world should not be a given in your life.

As an entrepreneur, you're in the lucky position of not being forced to trade life and its possibilities for a paycheck. You do have the control and can decide to take some of it back. Or to change the way you work so that it's not so burdensome that it causes unhappiness. Or to stop shortchanging yourself by rejecting opportunities for happiness right now in return for more money later. I discovered that trap after I made money from the product I made while at university. The Adii with the successful business could not trade the money for the happy, fully lived experiences I could have had as an eighteen-, nineteen-, or twenty-year-old.

Society has made it easy for us to trade happiness for money. And it's easy to believe that's the "way of things." But our approach to making money and our love of it combine to be destructive and unnatural to us. Instead of defaulting to a "more money is good" assumption, begin choosing intentionally when it is really worth it to pursue money instead of happiness in the moment in which you find yourself.

Happiness

Many of us entrepreneurs find the moment of now elusive. We tend to constantly be looking forward to the future, rushing into it at all times with a hard pace of action. And then, as we look at measurements and study them, we look at snapshots of the past, reviewing what was going on back then, trying to gain insights that will help us in the future. Between the past and future, the present is a blur. We don't like to live there. Yet, as American artist and poet Cleo Wade points out, "The only way we can make the most of our lives is to make the most of our moments."

Mindfulness is the hardest challenge. We struggle to still our minds because it's so much easier to constantly be running, applying a force in the same direction with momentum supporting your trajectory. It's far harder to literally sit still and reverse some of that momentum in our minds to bring us back into the present.

It's only in the context of the present, though, that you have the opportunity to have a constructive moment.

Happiness isn't a fleeting instant of joy or excitement or a "good time." It isn't even a string of those. Happiness is a sense of well-being, of purpose, of meaning, of being right with yourself and living as close as you can to your own nature instead of going against it. You can build that in your life when you make the most of your moments.

I found the sense of well-being and purpose as I began shifting things to make my business life-profitable. First, I learned to understand and view my entrepreneurial journey as something bigger than the business itself. My business had a larger purpose, that is, my life and my family. When I began making changes to the way I worked to honor that purpose, it became purer. My business was becoming more aligned with me, serving my purpose—instead of my life serving the business. And the life-first mental shift created a perspective that helped me to keep investments of time and energy in my business proportional to my larger life and family.

If life is always going to be the bigger thing, and work is only a part of life, then I don't have to get so caught up in that one challenging thing or that one bad moment. I can reorient my perspective and say, "You know what? This is going to be impermanent. Things are going to shape up one way or another, and I can focus on myself and on making the most of the moment. I can focus more on the people around me. I can try and have a meaningful life regardless of this business thing. I could lower the heat on myself and make more of my moments by valuing the opportunities in that small space of now."

There is no way to build a life-profitable business in a single moment. It requires multiple good moments where you intentionally make good decisions, moments where you're having the right conversations, meeting the right people, and figuring out how to best work with those people. Business tends not to care about those individual moments in favor of all of them together adding up to something down the road. Make the most of every single moment, every single day.

Quantity of time can't ensure the quality of time spent. Quality happens in the intentional use of moments to their best effect. If you can be the truest version of yourself, show up at work every single day, do meaningful work, and then have a meaningful life in addition to that, that's making the most of every moment, every day.

INTENT ON INTENTIONAL INTENTION

It's important to slow down and focus on moments, not only for the sake of living in a state of quality, but because if we don't, our conditioning can easily take over. We've been conditioned over the course of our lifetimes to live our lives as an adjunct to work and to confuse the pursuit of money with the pursuit of happiness. And we have been taught to believe that success comes through carrying out a certain formula involving unsustainable practices such as working sixty-hour weeks. If it were true that plugging yourself into a formula brings success, then failure rates wouldn't be so high. We must slow down to focus on moments to consciously reject the social constructs we've inherited and actually choose how we live.

Set your intentions for your time according to what you believe is most important to a life well lived right now, with your whole being as the context, all things rooted in the field of your possibilities. With that, you can begin to move toward a life-profitable business model, redistributing time, attention, and energy.

Remember, where you spend time, you spend heartbeats, and those are finite. Start to look at time in terms of these finite heartbeats. Your heartbeats are your own personal timekeeper of your mortality, the measure of time when you are present. And when you aren't, time will still pitilessly roll forward.

This is a serious and profound consideration. Issues of mortality call for reflection and sobriety. If you believe you "must" work a certain way, "must" dedicate as much of your life's time to work as possible, "must" let it command your attention, you are not free. How can you be? Your life doesn't belong to you. You must reclaim your freedom and then exercise it by making intentional choices instead of defaulting to the dogma of the entrepreneurial archetype. Choices must be made in light of your mortality and an intention to have a full and meaningful life right now.

Being an entrepreneur is *one* of the ways you express yourself. If you have been narrowing yourself in order to exclusively play that role, you have likely been feeling a great burden and sense of burnout. It feels as though "everything" depends on that role because it is the biggest or only thing in your life in terms of your fidelity. If you fail, it will feel like "everything" will be ruined. If you had a wider range of expression, it would not feel so risky to make changes to your business in favor of life profitability.

Let's not only exercise the muscle of being an entrepreneur. Let's also exercise the muscle of being a good mom or dad, of being a good friend or community leader or an author or a runner or a wine snob. Let's rediscover the ways that your life can be lived again if you stop amputating pieces of it to feed to your business. You've been dying for your business, but what is worth living for? We'll start to find it by looking within during the next chapter.

REFLECTION

*"In everything that you do, pause and
ask yourself if death is a dreadful thing
because it deprives you of this."*
—Marcus Aurelius, *Meditations*

What have you lost already? Is it "freedom"?

CHAPTER THREE

LIFE-PROFITABLE VALUES

THE PRIORITY OF THE SELF

i can only give to you
what i have already given to myself
i can only understand the world
as much as i understand myself

—Yung Pueblo

W e can only give what we already have. If I give myself permission to dream, I can share those dreams with you. If I give myself time to build strength, I can then later lend you my strength. If I expose myself to all manner of experiences, I can listen and contribute from a broader perspective than if I hadn't. But we entrepreneurs tend not to give ourselves such things, favoring our businesses instead. We cannibalize our lives for it; in turn, we cannibalize ourselves.

Naturally, we become hollowed out and end up with little left to give. We especially have little left to give to ourselves, even if we realize we ought to, no matter the pressure all around to be a "proper" entrepreneur, a single-minded, hard-driving, never-stop, go, go, go go-getter.

I did the same. After the success and sale of WooThemes, I'd been determined to make Conversio, my second business, another success. It meant a lot to me—proving that I wasn't a one-hit wonder, off on another entrepreneurial journey where I'd captain another endeavor to rich waters. I wanted to show myself I could do it, that my successful maiden voyage with WooThemes wouldn't be my only business accomplishment.

And so I got to paddling. I put my back into it and all my best focus. My mind was always racing, seeing challenges and overcoming them, finding opportunities and seizing them, making plans and executing them. I was on fire, fueled by my determination. It was go-time all the time, and there I was steering the boat, but mostly paddling, paddling, furiously paddling, sacrificing other parts of my life.

And then I succeeded. I looked up, took a breath, and found myself at sea, alone in an ocean, just me and the business.

It was like a spell was broken. The wind left my sails. I felt a sense of "now what?" and I didn't have an answer. The business was still there. The business was healthy. The business was still growing. Nothing had fundamentally changed in the business. Everything had fundamentally changed within me.

I'd achieved the goal, and that was great, but it didn't hold the value I thought it would. It didn't feel meaningful, and it didn't fill me up. It was just something to tick off. Check—I'm a successful entrepreneur, again. It was too small, too narrow to fill the whole of me, and I felt empty.

I know you've faced this sort of moment, or maybe many moments like this, on your entrepreneurial journey, times when discontent settles in where satisfaction was supposed to go. *What's gone wrong?* we ask ourselves. Or maybe, *What's wrong with me?* We all end up here. It's bound to happen when we get in the business of business first, life second, instead of insisting our ventures turn a life profit.

Facing this in the past, you probably chose a new path to a new goal, a shiny one that seems worthwhile, and then you got back in the boat and started paddling again. Action is your default, so it feels right to do this. Doing something and going somewhere also fits the entrepreneurial mold we've inherited. You can find a lot of reasons to justify doing again what you have just discovered leaves you empty: you don't like taking rest stops; you need to be in the game; your original goals weren't grand enough; more, always more is what drives successful businesses.

Don't do it. You're only going to paddle yourself further out to sea. Eventually, your burnout will be so acute that you'll consider abandoning ship. Your choices will seem narrowed down to two: keep the business or don't keep the business. You'll be looking at it through the lens of the sunk-cost fallacy, thinking:

> *Where should I push forward now? Should I push forward for another year or two? Just get the thing to some kind of finish line and exit?*
>
> *Or should I just quit right now, even knowing how I'll be judged in the eyes of my peers, my customers, and the broader public? I was going to be successful. I had all this bravado, maybe even arrogance, just to stand up and say, well, I'm going to change the status quo. I'm going to create something of value here. And now here I find myself, lost and empty.*
>
> *So, what now?*

I found myself there with Conversio—burnt out and feeling everything there had lost its meaning. But I was also tied to this thing in various ways, so I had to find a way to move forward again. I had to find new meaning, new purpose, a new plan without quitting completely. And this time I would not give myself a shiny new goal on the horizon and keep sailing out into a setting sun.

You're not going to do that either. As an entrepreneur who measures success according to life profitability, you won't make that mistake. "For what will it profit a man if he gains the whole world and forfeits his soul?" That warning has particular relevance for us entrepreneurs.

This time, instead of business as usual, we're going to see our discontent, burnout, and fatigue as a signal to challenge our default ways of coping, which are not working anyway, and transition into new ways of working. Doing this is a challenge and an opportunity, and that suits our entrepreneurial spirits because we know how to rise to those. We are going to be the entrepreneurs of our lives. And of course, that begins with you.

LIFE AS SELF-EXPRESSION

Naturally, the more you understand yourself, the clearer your options and choices become. They will represent you, and by choosing one course of action or another, you communicate who you are and what you stand for. The more you redistribute time and energy in your business to make it life-profitable, the more your business will communicate you as well. We make statements in how we clothe ourselves, showing others who and what we're about—say, dressed for hiking versus formally, in a fuzzy blue sweater or a sturdy white cotton shirt. So, too, do our business and business actions tell the world about us. It's all ultimately an expression of who we are.

That makes it all the more important to really think about your values and what you truly treasure. If you don't consciously put them at the center, it's all too easy to be in reaction mode all the time, acting on things that are urgent but not actually important to you. If you discover you value time with your children above all else but consistently interrupt time with them to take an important email, you are expressing something misaligned with your true self. You are saying children come second to you. (And over time, your children will likely come to believe that, because you expressed that by your distraction.)

I used to be that person. I was so very involved with parenting, trying to multitask, with the business always at hand by phone, changing a diaper with my mind mostly elsewhere, thinking about my company. Instead of watching a TV show with the family, I would be working in front of the TV, laptop open. We were all in the same room, but I was actually preoccupied with my occupation. Just as I had in my university days, I was shortchanging life.

One day, my wife, Jeanne, pointed out that I was managing everything in my life, coordinating it and organizing it to suit my business. Of course I was doing that—I thought I had to arrange things that way. I had to work hard and work long to be an "entrepreneur." It was the way things were. But Jeanne was pointing out a problem: I was managing everything in my life, coordinating it and organizing it to suit my business—including my children.

It was a shocking insight. The way I behaved did not portray a family man, even though that was who I considered myself to be.

I had really wanted a family. So much so that, instead of indulging some exciting hobby or travel adventures thanks to WooThemes' growing success, Jeanne and I quickly started a family after we got married. Being a dad, having a family—those were the most important reasons for starting a business, the why behind it, the value that served as my compass. I would have flexibility to give my family, I reasoned; I could take a week off to spend with them. Back then, the business was just a little baby dragon, having not yet grown into the ravenous dragon it was becoming. And now, there I was, working in front of the TV, changing diapers with phone at hand.

If you'd asked me back then, "Adii, who are you?" I would have given you some kind of biography or history of what I'd done to get to that point. I might have told you some things that I understood about my personality, good or bad. And I would have used a combination of labels: "I'm an entrepreneur and a family man." But observers evaluating my decisions on a week-to-week, month-to-month, year-to-year basis could be forgiven for questioning how much of a family man I actually was. This was unacceptable.

Jeanne challenged me to start thinking about the things I valued and how they were manifesting in my life right now. If you find, as I did, that you are not manifesting your values, you must find the disconnect. If you say, "My family is my highest value," but actions don't back that up, there's obviously a gap you need to bridge. That bridge will be built with life-profitable business decisions and actions based on the life-profitable value of the self.

You simply must take yourself into account. Here at your starting point, take the time to see your current circumstances as a chance for a study in your own character. Who are you? Being yourself is the most natural and the easiest for you to sustain. Stop contorting yourself and your life to suit the business, and instead let the business be part of how you show the real you.

BE SELF-CENTERED

Everything you've ever done started first from inside you. Impulsively or deliberately, your inside world shapes your outside world. The self is where you have the most influence and control. The self is where you find all your natural resources, the riches with which to create your life as you want it. But that can't happen if you are living outside yourself.

To access your own resources and control them, you must be self-centered in a good way. By being centered on yourself, you can live out your best and truest strengths, channeling them to best effect. This gives you the highest chance of success in all aspects of your life. Remember, you're the context. If you were a fish, you'd swim; if you were a giraffe, you'd eat from treetops; if you were the wind, you'd blow things around and be great at it. But you're you. Be self-centered. Everything ripples outward from that.

Step one is stepping back, winding down, stopping. Feel your self right now. You are here.

It's hard. Society rewards constant motion, forward momentum, and forward facing. And as entrepreneurs, we're trained, often by necessity, to move fast and do, do, do, go, go, go. It feels dangerous to stop, like we won't be able to find our place again. But you will. And if you've built momentum, the hamster wheel will keep turning, even without you. The world will keep spinning right on its axis if you just take ten minutes, one hour, one weekend for yourself. Doing this gives you an opportunity to just be, to think your own thoughts, to consider what you really wish you could do, those things you'd do if you weren't chained to the business beast with its constant demands. Here's your chance to break away.

If you've refused freedom for a long time, you might not have any idea anymore what doing you looks like. Like many of us in the West, you might have confused who you are with what you do—in your case, entrepreneur. But we're each larger and deeper than our business. There are whole worlds inside us, too much for a business to express, even if your business is one (merely one) of your life's passions. We're going to make a shift from "I am what I do" to "I do what I am." Living in that self-centered way, you'll be purer, more at peace, happier, stronger.

When you step back and step away, aim for a shift in perspective. That means putting yourself in a different context, a nonbusiness context. Was there a book you wanted to read, a movie you wanted to see, a catch-up conversation you wish you could have with a friend you're starting to lose touch with? Looking into your center, you have a chance to get to know yourself again by what you crave. From there, you can find what you value. Values are key.

REMEMBERING YOUR WHY

When I checked that box of having accomplished a second successful business, I discovered the motivation that drove my action was proving to myself I could do it again. But once done, the wind just left my sails. My boat sat on this vast open ocean, and I didn't know quite where to navigate or why. If I picked any direction, why would I go there? Only I could find the answer, and it had to be an answer that had lasting value to me—not in the framework of the outside world. I needed to reframe what my incentive and motivation and inspiration looked like for the business from the inside out before I did anything else.

The Japanese have a concept called *ikigai* that finds your reason for being at the center of the overlapping forces of life and of self. Life's basic necessities require us to be paid, so choosing a career or business in a field that matches your innate skills makes sense. But you'll truly thrive if your passion and values overlap with those practical considerations and you also know you are contributing something the world needs. It's the sweet spot of meaning, the why that truly justifies what you do in life. It not only keeps people alive longer because they enjoy life; it keeps people alive longer because they're actually living. Finding meaning on a daily basis supports longevity. And doing meaningful things motivates you to keep on doing them: they become sustainable activities.

Unfortunately, we entrepreneurs see opportunities everywhere, and sometimes the capitalist part of our brain takes over. We get fired up, and it feels like passion. We take on an entrepreneurial challenge only to find ourselves living in a space outside of our true values. It wasn't passion after all, so much as it was excitement. When you look back at why you started your business in the first place, you might find it had less to do with meaning and more to do with ego or adventuring, more to do with checking off a box. Does the reason you had in the beginning or even last year still align with who you are today and who you are at your core?

And is your why still so relevant that, when you consider the life costs to you and those close to you, the business is still worth doing? There's always an opportunity cost of doing one thing versus another. In every decision, we trade one thing for another. It's important to compare these costs to the reasons you had at the beginning of your entrepreneurial journey to get a sense of where you need to make shifts in how you do business. For me, proving I was a "real entrepreneur" in the sense that I knew how to make successful businesses had hollowed me out. It was not an adequate reason to continue in a business.

Perhaps you, like most of us, started a business to get off the hamster wheel and out of the hamster cage but now know you've just traded one cage for another. You think, *At least it's my cage*, but trading cages isn't the reason you started in business. You wanted less cost to your life, the flexibility to live according to your values, with an income that let you pursue your passions. Perhaps you wanted to travel or to have the flexibility to homeschool your children or to pursue the cello and join your local community orchestra. But that hasn't happened. The business is paying the bills for your material lifestyle—the house, the cars, the schools—but that's all it's doing. It doesn't buy you the time to pursue the passions you thought it would.

When you find, as I did, that your original justification for becoming an entrepreneur doesn't align with who you are and what you deeply value, you must reinject meaning into your journey. Think of it as a new leg of that expedition and not as something you didn't get right. Much of this misalignment between meaning and what you actually do stems from a lack of awareness of what we're doing when we start out, especially because we are following an entrepreneurial template.

And following it got you somewhere, right? But the you part of it is missing. We need to align your reasons for being with your business's reason for being. How can the business empower your reasons for being—if not in the work itself, at least in what it enables you to do? When I took my family on my work trips, my business supported Adii, the family man. Perhaps you can reenvision how or what your business does and for whom.

Of course, expect some trial and error as you find ways to express your values in tandem with your business. My combined work and family trips, for instance? Some worked better than others. The Bali trip was great. But sometimes work got out of its time-and-place box and intruded on the family leisure part of the trip. Then, of course, I'd feel like I shorted my family.

But we're entrepreneurs! We can think of ways to do it better next time. On one work trip to the United States, my friend and team member brought his wife, and I brought my wife and kids. While my teammate and I worked, our families vacationed together. After the work was complete, we tacked extra days on to the trip so that we all got our vacation time. Instead of me being on another continent, my family and I were together and got to holiday. The point is, find solutions for things interfering with life profitability, and find opportunities to practice it.

As entrepreneurs, once we set our brain to seeing opportunities, we find many. But this time, we're going to weigh any possible action on opportunities against our abiding values. Beyond looking at what the original dreams were when you started your business, ask yourself why *those* dreams. It will point to something deeper, something that matters to you. Remember that *you* are the context of a life-profitable business.

A NEW STARTING POINT OF SELF

Business starts when you find yourself dissatisfied with the status quo. And now we're here again, feeling strong dissatisfaction—even pain—thanks to the status quo of the way we've been living out our businesses. It takes a healthy ego to take a risk and chart a new entrepreneurial direction, whether you're starting a business or embarking on a new leg of your journey, but being used to risk, some of you probably already imagine a few ways to build in life profitability. Thinking them over, the executive function in your brain will probably want to make it all about the measurement world. Rein that in, always mindful of the larger context for your business, which is you.

When I found myself at sea with Conversio, without a clear direction and looking for meaning, I began thinking about Conversio in the larger scheme of things. A big part of Conversio's journey had always been about certain business values. We wanted Conversio to try to be a change agent, at least within our own e-commerce ecosystems, and to take a softer, kinder, better approach to marketing. So, as I tried to reorient myself, I thought, *Well, okay, we have the foundations of a good business here. And we've got these very aspirational things that we want to do. Looking outward to the world, we could try to create values-based change that ripples out into the industry.* This felt like important and meaningful work that would give our efforts purpose in a certain direction.

But that didn't work. We weren't making progress in those things that furthered our aspirations. I realized that those things were too far removed from my influence and impact. It was like trying to make an impact on the opposite bank of a vast river by throwing stones with all my might and falling short. I realized, though, that I could impact the other side if I started with myself. If I entered the river, I'd move the water. It would ripple out from me in concentric circles.

By starting with myself and those closest with me, my influence could ripple out to my team members, and then perhaps to our customers, the market, and the wider world. If I worked to create impact in the circle of self, I had a much better chance of "making a difference" because I had more control, or at least more influence, and thus more chance to create growth in myself and my immediate surroundings. It's a matter of where I actually am likely to have the most influence. The closer I stay to myself, the more likely it is that I will actually get the thing that I want.

Likewise, I want you to draw inward before moving outward—to find the why behind your dream and see how you can manifest that in yourself and your immediate surroundings. Instead of trying to shoot far into a context outside yourself where there are multiple considerations that you may be blind to or that take coordination, stay within those concentric circles of self, others, and business to get there.

If I wanted to achieve something that's outside my realms of influence at this stage, I probably would need to take some kind of stairstep approach to putting myself in that new context sometime in the future. But in that case, I still have to start with where and who I am today.

SUSTAINABILITY

Typically, we entrepreneurs burn the candle at both ends, dashing through our days hoping we accomplish everything we must before the wax is melted and the fire sputters out. It makes no sense, though, to power through our journey without refueling. Entrepreneurship is a way of work life, not a one-time jog where we hope to reach some apex before we drop. If you are going to be on this journey for "as long as it takes," you must figure in sustainability and renewal. Recognize the reality of your reality: you are an entrepreneur. You will always be trying to change the status quo, strive, and follow the light of ambition up the hill. It's imperative to be properly outfitted.

Before now, the way you have outfitted yourself has been inadequate. Instead of taking on the proper supplies and developing the muscle to carry it, your solution to a strenuous climb has been to carry less. Climbing the mountain with its rarified views and inadequate air, you've begun throwing the supplies you did pack into the crevasses. You think less weight will help you and give you room to move. But it is, in fact, the opposite. To summit, you must have on hand sustaining things. You need nourishment; you need air; you need warmth; you need light.

In other words, sustaining yourself means sustaining your journey. It is best for you and therefore everything you touch that you ensure your best efforts. The exact elements you need for sustainability are specific to your context. Those elements don't include notions of future payoffs such as money, reputation, fame, and power. Dreaming of one or more of those may keep you looking forward, but they won't keep you moving forward indefinitely. If you manage to arrive, you'll be empty with all the marrow of meaning burned out. To keep that from happening, you must seek out meaningful experiences, nourishing pursuits, and see to regular rest and unplugging. These must be your priority.

The word *priority* comes from the concept of being earlier. Priority is something that factually came first and has rank and precedence. You came before your business. Your needs take precedence over the business's needs. It's just a fact. Humans must tend to their humanness—their mortality—or their humanness and mortality flounder. No running your business then.

And priority shouldn't have a plural and didn't take one on until we tried to be more "productive" during the mid-twentieth century. How can more than one thing be first? Juggling "priorities" is another ill-conceived idea attached to the entrepreneurial archetype. I'm not suggesting that during your day you won't attend to more than one important issue. But for sustainability, you must center yourself around what it is to be you. Your welfare comes before the welfare of your business. Your highest value can then be the organizing principle for your days. Meaning and self-actualization will transcend lesser considerations. Remember, you are the field from which the universe plants its possibilities, and yours is a multidimensional world of wholesomeness and shape.

Of course, I know this is easier said than done when you've been holding on to your business with a white-knuckle grip. Your business is volatile and demanding, and it's frightening to think about easing up your grip bit by bit—as heart-stopping as movie scenes where someone may or may not let go one hand to grab hold of the arm that can pull them to safety. And sometimes the character can't grab the saving hand, no matter the exhortations of the other characters and you, watching at home, hands sweating as you anticipate their fall. They can't grab the saving hand, because when you've been holding on so long, it's as if the natural mechanics of the body, the mind, and the heart go into spasm. It's hard to release this thing when you've held it so dearly for so long. But you must. Otherwise you cannot take yourself in hand.

For me, I had to start releasing my death grip out of necessity. Big parts of my personal life had begun to fall apart. And then later, I had to lay people off. I felt burnt out and overmatched by the demands of the business. I thought, *This shit is just way too hard*, and I felt like throwing everything away, just letting go and letting it be over.

The solution wasn't to sell, though. I knew I'd just start a new business and end up in the same place. I realized I had to do business sustainably; it had to stop costing me life, and, in fact, it had to profit my life. I made the decision to embark on a process that focused on having a financially healthy business, controlling growth, and doing it in a way that could create more time for me. I made a business that could sustain me with practices that put me in the center, living out my life.

It took awareness and attentiveness, and intention and purposefulness practiced on a daily basis. For instance, I learned to meditate to pull myself back from the future orientation so that I could make the most of my moments. I did it daily and began a streak that lasted almost a year. I still meditate. If you are in as deep a hole as I was in, you've got healing to do. Self-triage. Start doing things that not only nourish you but heal you. Build in time for your healing bit by bit. Add a passion for who you are to the passion you have for what you do. Persist in the art of shaping and managing yourself. You will grow and come to fruition, yielding a return on yourself. When the journey is about yourself, self-investment gives you the greatest chance to bend your strengths toward success.

So far, trying to envision your business as a function of you instead of the other way around has probably revealed some insights about how far you are from that—from a place where your life represents your best universe of possibility. Some of you may be in such a toxic relationship with your business, suffering so much damage that an intervention is necessary. That can mean some difficult decisions and some courageous action. You might be in a seemingly impossible position because it's not always possible to quit all the things causing trouble right now in favor of a new approach.

But it's always possible to start where you are today and from there try to incrementally change the context of how you operate your business. You can stop it from claiming your life. You can reclaim your life for yourself. You can cut out the things that don't serve you and transition into things that do. The sooner the better. Starting that transition process, even if it's just in your head and heart, is very important. You can begin taking steps thereafter to say, "You know what, I can't unwind this thing completely in the short-term. It's going to take me six or twelve months. But this is where I'm going, and this is why I'm going there. And this is the reason why I need to transition out of this part of my life: I need to make life livable."

In the next chapter, we're going to examine some ways to become the entrepreneur of your life.

REFLECTION

*"Burnout happens at work or at home
when the meaning goes out of what you
are doing but you have too much invested
to stop and take notice. When you were
wholehearted, you could do, achieve, give
everything and there was energy to spare."*
—Dina Glouberman, *The Joy of Burnout*

Crowding out everything else in favor of business has left no room even for you. How much space is there for you to be wholehearted? How much space is there for you to be free? How much space in your day, in your mind, in your heart? The you that exists regardless of your business's existence—where is the space *that* you lives?

CHAPTER FOUR

MODELS OF LIVING PROFITABLY

THE SELF

Find your significance within yourself.
Within your own sphere of power—that is
where you have the greatest consequence.

—Epictetus

You cannot escape yourself. It is a blessing and a curse, your doom and your salvation.

I lived that during the times when, as I told you last chapter, I once more achieved entrepreneurial success through Conversio and felt a surge of, well, nothing really.

I didn't chase the next shiny object or scale up my goals, an impulse we entrepreneurs often give in to. Instead of thinking my milestone achievement must not have been interesting enough or grand enough, I stopped and let myself feel the discomfort of my emptiness. If I had run forward to enlarge my success, graduating from my row-boat on the ocean to a sailboat and then a yacht, I would still be out there alone, disappointed, and empty where joy was meant to be.

Scaling up without life profitability would have only likewise scaled up the extent of my self-neglect, a whole yacht's worth of it. The hollowness would have grown so large, so vast that its silence would have felt like the scream of a ghost, my own being grown pale in the shadow of my business, with its endless entrepreneurial labors.

No amount of commercial success can plaster over the cracks of self. You carry the state of yourself everywhere you go. The worst of you stays close, but the best of you does too. If you are your own worst enemy at times, you are at all times your own best hope.

If you are suffering as I did, having hollowed yourself out to feed your endlessly hungry business, your salvation is to choose actions that refill you with your own being. Though we can talk about certain models for doing that, only you know the contours of yourself—the depth of you, the shape of you, the flow of what it is to be you. Only you control the vast territory of yourself and your psychology.

You are its explorer, the conqueror of its demons, the sage who understands its truths, the healer who can mend wholeness from fracture.

Wander the internal landscape that is you, adopting practices that best promote your well-being. Do that until your being flows free again and your living becomes self-expression. Now is where you act to make that shift from "I am what I do" to "I do what I am."

In short, you're going to model yourself.

EXPLORATION

You are the foundation of a life-profitable business, so you must purposefully get reacquainted with a version of yourself that you might remember from a freer, happier time in life. You may have memories of that you, or perhaps you may run into yourself every so often when you do something novel and see yourself react spontaneously and naturally.

You need that version of yourself, the adaptable explorer who can make a plan and then depart from the plan when a better path opens up. Finding your particular keys to life profitability is always going to be "choose your own adventure," so being in touch with a healed, whole, true you will let you choose the right doors to open. Learning to manage your mind and heart, applying them in the right direction, experimenting with the right force and energy toward choosing yourself—this is going to take openness and willingness. And it's going to take finding things vital to your sense of feeling "right" in the world. Vital things mean vitality. Their significance beckons—it's an attraction that pulls your energy toward them when the entropy of the past would sap you and keep you on your rutted path.

Even if you are in enough pain that you believe you'd do anything short of shuttering your business to take back your life, there's no particular anything to do until you go inside yourself and start to explore the terrain. To get returns on yourself, you'll need to invest in finding your inner resources and take care of your own psychological, emotional, and physical life. What you are has consequence in the world. That means that what you are is significant to everything else. Growing as a person increases your personal currency. Then you can spend those returns on yourself in ways that have significance.

Significance

Significance is important to your sense of efficacy and meaning. Putting life first doesn't mean that you only regain the happy, fun, light things that you sacrificed to your business. Life first also means muscularity, weightiness, and gravity. There are things you would do no matter how hard—like your business. Unfortunately, building a business is not, in itself, truly significant. So, what is? What is so important you'd sacrifice life and energy to it? Family comes to mind, causes too, or perhaps mastery of a musical instrument, a sphere of knowledge, or a physical discipline. What makes the costs worth it? If you willingly would do these things and do them regularly, you've likely found significance. It points you toward your values. Despite their cost, things of true significance still net you profit.

The significance of the self, then, is not only your own inherent importance but standards that curate things of significance for you. Recognizing them gets you a step closer to living as you truly are. For me, one example of significance is my desire to learn, to evolve, to constantly develop myself. I will always come back to learning regardless of what I'm actually working on today, tomorrow, or next week. Whether I'm working at my business, this book, running—I will always come back to my significant questions: How can I learn more? How can I put that learning to work? How can I evolve?

Don't look for significance in material objects. That takes you back to the measurement world and eventual burnout. But if you find yourself thinking, *My home is significant to me*, look behind it. Perhaps it is not your home but the safety it represents for your family and the memories you make there. Then the significance becomes more about family ties and closeness and belongingness. Look around at the things you own and ask yourself what they say about you. You may find important answers.

For entrepreneurs buried in work, thought experiments can provide a straightforward tool to unearth information about yourself and your life. In 2017, I had to lay off two team members and restructure my business. The decision needed thought and soul-searching, not only in terms of the business but in terms of what it all meant for and to me. During this time and in the aftershock, I began reviewing what I value. The process grounded me, and my decisions going forward grew out of that. I used a book called *The Values Factor* by Dr. John Demartini. He asked readers to answer thirteen questions:

1. How do you feel about your personal space?
2. How do you spend your time?
3. How do you spend your energy and where do you feel energized?
4. How do you spend your money?
5. Where do you have the most order and organization?
6. Where are you most reliable, disciplined, and focused?
7. What do you think about and what is your most dominant thought? (In my notes, I added in brackets, "How do I want to live my life?")
8. What do you visualize and realize?
9. What is your internal dialogue? (That speaks to intention.)

10. What do you talk about in social settings? (In brackets, my note was "What makes me an extrovert?")
11. What inspires you?
12. What are your most consistent long-term goals?
13. What do you learn and read about most?

Even an untrained eye can begin to see personal patterns and leanings in looking over the answers to such questions. And if you make room in your head and schedule to explore, you'll likely begin to see more questions you ought to ask yourself. This isn't about doing an exercise so much as it is about building a values vocabulary, finding the language that speaks your meaning. Vocabulary drives awareness, and when we become aware of it, we begin to optimize and prioritize for it. We make space, work it into our actions.

Another way I started getting my bearings when I found myself in the middle of the ocean was to take a couple weeks to write down everything I did daily. I was trying to identify the things I liked or didn't like. What actually happened was that I found things that drained energy or cluttered my life, while other things or actions created energy and added space. Take note throughout your day. Becoming aware of what adds or subtracts from you and your life is an important first step in making the best use of yourself and your life.

And go back to the answers to the questions above through that same lens of adding or subtracting energy and space. You may find a starting point to immediately give yourself relief. If you know that creating a spreadsheet bogs you down and you come away spent, find a way to automate parts of it or delegate the task. If organizing your desk gives you a sense of calm and renewal, take that as a clue that you value harmony and order, perhaps simplicity.

Looking back, I can now see very clearly how my thought threads and considerations back then influenced many of the decisions I've made in the years since. I didn't figure everything out at the time, and you won't either. You don't need to. Your boat is in the middle of this vast open ocean. You only need to figure out the general direction in which you think you ought to go. A sense of direction is better than where you are now, which is completely lost. You just need some kind of answer, not the full answer. Something that starts looking as if it could be an answer helps you move forward again, away from this place of doldrums.

Resistance

Of course, you have to be ready and willing to start exploring. You should expect resistance. Some part of you will almost certainly put up a fight. As entrepreneurs, justifications for and against come easy. It's a talent that lets us challenge the status quo. I, for instance, am really good at mitigating opinions that don't make sense for where I am today—or for what I want to hear. I'm great at adding just that little bit of doubt into a conversation that throws the feedback givers off a little bit. But that ability can, of course, be misused. It's not hard to resist what I know to be true about a situation and about myself when I'm not quite willing to take that next step.

For instance, my talent for justification intervenes when I think about my physical well-being. "Life first" calls for health, yet I appreciate fine wine. I exercise a lot and regularly, but if I really wanted to reach my ideal peak of health and weight, the solution is to sample less wine. But fine wine is one of my hobbies, and the truth of the matter is that I want to indulge myself.

We want to indulge our businesses, too, and have done much more than is healthy. You must start being honest with yourself, becoming wise to your own ways. Resistance, like significance, points to something deeper about yourself. When you feel yourself resisting and rationalizing, you can take it as an opportunity to discover something. Why are you resisting? Are you avoiding something you'll have to do? Are you avoiding discomfort or pain? Are you afraid of losing control?

Losing control is a common fear for entrepreneurs. Typically, we overrely on ourselves, which makes us want to control all the things we do in business and their outcomes. We start believing that we are the only ones who can figure something out. We've attached way too much significance to what a single person can do. And I think we entrepreneurs have internalized that to a point where it is toxic.

We also tend to fear losing control of ourselves. We are supposed to be tough, tough enough to not feel discomfort and fear, or to be affected by self-doubt. We're supposed to be impervious to past injuries or even traumas. We think we can't afford all those feelings. We are callous to our internal needs, as if they are in the way.

But ignoring them just leads to hidden agendas, and these hidden motivations sometimes prop up resistance. For instance, we may secretly believe that we can fix past wrongs, fix our childhoods altogether, by being successful entrepreneurs. Many people think that success—whether it's measured in sheer amounts of money or writing a bestseller or curing cancer—will somehow make them whole. They might even feel like success will retroactively fix their traumas, as if everybody will come to their senses and apologize for wrongdoings. But that's likely a vain hope. And it's not life first right now. It's the past driving you, where your values should.

Hidden motivations and fears are another reason that you need space for yourself as someone distinct from entrepreneur. Oftentimes, to have a realization, you need to be exposed to something that stimulates an insight and growth. Maybe someone ventures over your path, or you read a thought-provoking book, or a good friend asks a truthful question that calls up deeper answers.

Maybe you use space away from business to reimagine your current reality. What if you did change up the length of your workday or how you get things done? What would happen if you gave yourself the freedom to do just one thing at a time and gained the simple peace of just that? Being open to yourself and life, and making the most of time right now, will give you the opportunity to achieve returns on yourself.

PRACTICES

Entrepreneurs crave freedom. We want to do our own thing, we want to do it our own way, and we'll choose when to do it.

Me too. I thought I hated structure until I had a young family. My kids behaved as kids do, random and unpredictable, noisy and quiet and then too quiet, laughing and crying and generally giving life an air of underlying chaos that could erupt at any moment, typically when you let your guard down. I couldn't plan and structure my way around them. I had to flow around them instead, adapting to their (usually) pleasant madness.

But constantly adapting made me see structure with new eyes. I realized that, yes, I like a certain amount of flexibility—maybe even optionality—but I actually do my best work and am at my most calm when I have some structure around me. Obviously, I still loved freedom; structure was not being imposed on me. I could create the structure, but it was structure nonetheless.

Habits or disciplines provide these sorts of self-imposed supporting frames for growth. They aren't rigid constructions walling you in. Instead, they're more like the architecture of a beehive, providing the spaces for life to take hold, to produce, to buzz with self-actualizing, self-fulfilling living. They are life-profitable structures.

For me, starting at the beginning and starting with myself, the core of this was really thinking through the cultivation of a certain set of habits, specifically habits that create space instead of taking up space. The idea of populating time with something that somehow makes more free space may sound contradictory or counterintuitive, but it's akin to the idea of spending a dollar but getting two back because it was an investment.

Or, to put it another way, plant one seed, end up with a tree full of apples, and from there, an orchard.

The Hour

One of the most significant space-creating habits I cultivated was carving out an hour a day for myself between five and six in the morning. For that hour, the only things I did were have a coffee, meditate fifteen to twenty minutes, and read one of the two or three books I was going through, whichever caught my fancy that morning.

I was relatively guaranteed that the kids would not wake up before six on most days. Which meant that the time before they woke up was generally the only hour in a day that I could truly carve out time just for myself. So I did, and did so religiously.

I was enabling myself to start my day in the calmest, most me-centric way possible, and not me in a selfish way. I was really just kind of waking up, unfolding from sleep inside and out, and just being alone with myself at least for the first hour. I didn't wear any hat, not dad or husband or entrepreneur. I wasn't wearing any uniform except my own skin, and I felt at home there. The more I gave myself that hour, the easier it was for my mind to stay with me in the present where I was instead of going off to be with my future work. I just spent that time naturally, as me, open to myself, full of my own being. And the habit became indispensable. In other words, I became indispensable to myself, and the me that evolved became indispensable to my larger life. Every day started as a good day, a good foundation. I carried that centered and strong mental space with me to everything that followed.

The time also gave me a chance to set an intention for the day, an intention centered on the self. Creating that hour's space and showing up to it every day reinforced the intention, and it strengthened as I repeated it from day to day. It had a profound effect on me. Habits that nourish do that. At first there is friction in starting the habit, but then it enlarges you and affirms your identity. Your brain wires itself and you experience an evolution of self from doing the habit over and over again.

Mindfulness

Practicing mindfulness has also had a profound effect on me, creating a noticeable difference in my life. It was the initial big change I made, learned as a way to address my anger, which, it turned out, was hypervigilance in disguise. You might be in the same state. My brain was constantly on fire, always ready for fight or flight. The impact was that I was thinking in the very short term instead of the slightly longer term about the challenges and issues I was facing. I'd feel like I just needed to fix this one thing tomorrow and then everything else was going to be fixed for the long term.

That hypervigilance leaked into the way I related to other human beings, and it affected my most significant relationships, including my marriage and close friendships. My sensitivity to things that looked like red flags was just off the charts. I couldn't stand down; everything required vigilance.

Constant fight-or-flight mode actually made me less ambitious and less adventurous as an entrepreneur. I felt like I had to avoid all the small mistakes. For instance, I overinvested in control as a way of saving money, trying to avoid all these small expenditures. Yes, I needed to turn the business around when we hit some rough times, but in hindsight it was penny wise, pound foolish to some extent. I was gripping tightly to so many things that I paid a heavy price personally. There's no way to even communicate the cost burden to me. Even though Conversio ultimately had a happy ending, I do wonder: if hypervigilance hadn't clipped my wings—if it hadn't dulled my ambition, my sense of adventure, my risk appetite, my ability to navigate unpredictability—could we have built a better or bigger business? Hypervigilance focused me on the wrong things; it made me less as an entrepreneur.

This is bound to happen when you have placed your center outside yourself and into the business where its survival begins to feel like life and death. In this state, there are no lived moments. Every moment is just a borrowed moment, a brief instant before something happens that you worry you'll need to react to. You begin scanning for threats, and in a self-fulfilling prophecy, you begin to find them. I could no longer see longer-term possibilities. I wasn't living in that universe.

Fortunately, modern science is now showing that mindfulness, that awareness of now, specifically meditation, can smooth the well-traveled, rutted tracks in your brain from past trauma or just conditioning. New tracks can emerge as new habits and thought patterns form. Being mindful of the present, not being pulled forward into "What's next? What's next? What's next?" begins to decentralize business and shift it toward its rightful place in your life.

And mindfulness also pulls you back from the "always more growth" mindset. That mindset urges you to do more as soon as possible. Instead of tilting that way, you're mindful of just being here in this moment, just being with yourself, comfortable or accepting discomfort for this minute right now.

In my meditation I focus on the breath work, which taught me how to be more mindful. It's not that I didn't meditate on a particular issue. For instance, some guided meditations might focus on gratitude for others. But focusing on breath, the breath right now going into my body, going out of my body—the sensation taught me how to be present in my present. The better I get at mindfulness, the more aware I am of how I feel in any given moment, and I can catch feelings before I just react to them.

For me, practicing meditation and mindfulness, change happened quickly—in just a couple of weeks. Sometimes it works like that: a single decision toward action can set you off on a new path, as mindfulness did for me. But mostly, make changes incrementally and expect incremental change. If you're on a furiously spinning hamster wheel, jumping off can cause injury. The better way, if you're the hamster, is to start running a little bit slower, and then slower and slower to get off safely. So right now, if you're imagining what you can do next, you can probably consider one or two new habits or disciplines, or a couple new ways of thinking that start to create a new kind of momentum that allows you to incrementally change your life toward a more life-profitable phase.

Journaling

I've always used writing as my own therapy. It eventually debuted in my morning routine about once a week as some form of journaling or morning pages. I discovered that writing things after I meditated was the most powerful. Already primed to be open to the moment, reflecting more readily yielded insights. Meanwhile, my deepest values stood ready to give meaning.

As ink flows out on a piece of paper, I find all these thoughts—these to-dos, issues, challenges, problems solved—they leave my mind. I feel peace, comfort, and security knowing that all of it has now been deposited on a piece of paper. As long as I don't lose the piece of paper, I don't have to worry about them again.

These notes also start to capture the trends of moods or issues you might not notice while living your busy life. If you see in the span of a month that there are fifteen entries and the majority of them mention depression or anxiety, that's something to pay attention to.

And reading between the lines, you can also start seeing issues and concepts that you've been wrestling with or exploring without even quite knowing it. You can then examine the reasons such things are relevant and important to you right now. Ask yourself "why" questions: *Why does this keep coming up? Why does it make me feel the way it does? Why now?* Such reflections are also just a type of meditation, a way to recalibrate yourself to your deeper being, to get in tune with yourself.

Trip Wires

As I was selling my share of WooThemes and before starting Conversio, I dabbled with a new business called PublicBeta. At the time, I hadn't developed any of the vocabulary that I use now to analyze what was happening inside me. But something was definitely wrong.

A team member asked me something simple, like "What color should this button on the website be?"

I couldn't answer. Instead, I felt completely overwhelmed and tired and angry. Even I could notice that I was in a state. At the time, I called it decision fatigue. I now understand there was something much greater happening: I was completely burnt out.

Nowadays, I don't wait for things to go so far wrong that I can't answer simple questions. As soon as I am short with anyone, whether in the business or with my family or people around me, I know it's an indication that something is off. Something has been tripped, and being short with someone is the alarm that something needs investigating.

Tiredness or lack of enthusiasm is another trip wire for me. After my morning's hour routine, I should be launching into my day on a good trajectory. But say that two or three hours into my day I find I'm tired, physically and mentally. I'm not feeling motivated. Things take more effort. It's time to take notice and see what's gone wrong, especially if that's happened two or three days in a row.

A related trip wire is not finding pleasure or energy where it normally would be. It used to be when that happened, I'd find fault with whatever had failed to bring on the expected feelings. But as I became more attuned to myself, down states became personal clues that I was getting further from myself than was good for me in some situation. In other words, something had me pulled outside my core, off my center of gravity.

Irritability, loss of pleasure, waking up and still being tired—these are common to overworked "out of body" entrepreneurs. It's tempting to think you're not coping well enough, as if you are showing weakness, when the reality is that you're just experiencing symptoms. If you are practicing things like journaling, you may be able to quickly pinpoint the cause. Maybe the cause will turn out to be just a temporary situation. But if not, the tripped wire is a signal to make an adjustment. Have you been taking the time to nourish yourself? Have you had enough regular downtime?

For me, when I've tripped a wire, I either read, write, meditate, or most often, go for a run. Movement is good for our brains, helping us to change our state of mind. If I had a long run in the morning and found myself really pissed off late in the afternoon, I would just go for a walk. If I choose to read, it has to be fiction, not some kind of self-improvement book or something business-related. You need an escape, something to move you to a new mental space. If your current space were serving you, there'd be no tripped wire.

Good Distractions

These self-feeding, constructive activities—writing, reading, running—are "good distractions." Far from pulling you dangerously out of the orbit of business, they help the business by helping you. For instance, 2016 was probably the best calendar year I ever experienced in business. It was also the year that I trained to run a marathon for the first time. I set myself a very ambitious goal to run a sub-four-hour marathon. I ran thirty to forty miles every week, putting in six to seven hours on the road. Before each run, there was prep time; after each run, there was recovery time. I practiced strength training and Pilates, and had regular sessions with a physiotherapist.

From where you sit, struggling to take any time away from your business, me spending upwards of a whole full-time job's worth of time on running must strike you as—well, words might fail you. But this good distraction meant my business wasn't the only outlet for my drive and ambition. To succeed, I had to slightly loosen my grip on the business, even when things weren't working out the way I wanted them to. Remember what I said about control interfering with my entrepreneurial traits earlier? Loosening a bit of control actually improved my performance.

And thanks to all that running, I spent 2016 tired. Some days I just didn't have the energy to put in extra work hours. Because I worked less, I let things just fall off my radar instead of trying to do it all myself. I wasn't that involved. I couldn't be.

Working less also meant accomplishing things at a slower rate. I wasn't ticking every single box in the order or in the manner or on the timeline that I probably would have done and maybe even should have done. They still got done, of course, but it turned out that even if I didn't rev my engine for every little thing, it worked out. And I didn't need to scrutinize every single thing either.

I wasn't doing these things because I couldn't. I was just tired. I had this other thing that I was doing. It turned out better for me, and it turned out better for the business.

The year 2017 was a different story. Conditions had changed. I had to lay off two team members and restructure the business during that dark period at the end of 2017. I turned to reading and writing poetry, trying to put words to what I was feeling:

Working on these words has been a distraction and indulgence. The process has been a beacon to my personal version of what enlightenment could feel like. Suspended among the words I can float, vacillating between comfort and discomfort.

Writing was not an escape. It just put healthy space between me and the business. It gave me breathing room and, thus, perspective. It wasn't just a good distraction, but a healthy one as well.

LIGHTHOUSES

Sometimes you're too close to a situation to notice you've tripped a wire. It's then that other people may help you out. In my life, my wife, Jeanne, does that for me. I call her the omnipresent observer. We've been married for over a decade; we're also co-parents, and I am open to her as my partner. We have familiarity and rapport with each other, along with respect and trust. She has an incredibly helpful tact when she floats something in a gentle, kind way and says, "You know what? It seems like something is off" or "Hey, you know what? Today you snapped at the kids twice for seemingly small things. What's up?"

Those observations are often hard to hear. But it's worth it to be open to them. Someone just close enough to see and care, but separate enough to provide objectivity can steer you back on course. When you're in the boat in the middle of the ocean with a storm raging around you, you can't see beyond the waves. Whereas that person running the lighthouse is trying to call you closer to the shore and out of the storm. It's very hard to be the observer of yourself.

My best friend in the world, De Wet, is another person who shines a light for me. Though conventional business wisdom says don't work with friends, it has worked out for us. He became my second-in-command at Conversio. So we, too, have familiarity and rapport, mutual respect and trust. But he also had the vantage point of seeing me at work in a day-to-day context and understood the challenging or relevant issues in the business.

Both he and Jeanne know me well and have empathy. When they bring things up, it is with concern on a personal level. It's not just "Hey, you seem irritated today," but more of "Hey, I can see you're irritated. That conversation we had with that supplier earlier on really seemed to bother you. Do you want to talk about it?"

It's a supportive prompt. Sometimes it's validation, like "Hey that was a really shitty meeting," which can be great for entrepreneurs. We often feel alone. For me, looking back at the journey with Conversio, hiring my best friend and having him grow into being that second-in-command is one of the top three decisions I made with the business.

To make sure our relationships stay strong, we make a habit of dedicating time to them. Jeanne and I go out every week, with no work or children talk. The point is to foster intimacy, to really connect with another significant human being in your life. When we were working together, De Wet and I would take weekly lunches, spending the first half doing some work and the second half talking about whatever. We would have a beer and then we would go back to work afterward.

Non-transactional interactions can be sparse for entrepreneurs. It's important to make a habit of them. For me, putting preplanned things into every single week meant that even if things went a little haywire, I would have self-correction opportunities waiting. I had a support system built into my schedule, regardless of my ability to remember to use them.

Relationships with those meaningful others satisfy our need for connection and belonging. These often-neglected connections nourish us. Take the time. Create boundaries for your business. Don't let it encroach.

EXPRESSIONS OF SELF

You might be interested to know that French philosopher Michel Foucault is credited with the first mention of "entrepreneur of the self," at least in public mainstream literature, in the 1970s. He did so in a published collection of lectures called *The Birth of Biopolitics*. He argued that the concept of entrepreneur of self was rooted in what he called *new liberalism*, a term coined after World War II to describe the idea that you can be the best that you can be. There were many opportunities to grab, and you had the freedom to pursue them. You had some limitations in terms of rules and regulations in society, but mostly there were opportunities that let you achieve your best. If you wanted to invest in yourself, then there'd be some return on that investment. It's interesting to note that this idea of self-development was immediately grafted onto an economic framework, or set of measures, and that intertwining has been difficult to untangle ever since.

Foucault foresaw this. After he had become known for writing about this entrepreneur of the self, he started speaking and writing about care of the self instead. And that became his primary inquiry, almost a complete shift in his philosophy. He began exploring how we are socialized and wondering what other ways of being were available—the other opportunities we could grab that would let us realize our best selves.

He recognized a tendency to fall into automatic pilot—to give expression to a narrative that does not serve us. He spoke about Seneca, who had this simple suggestion that every single morning when you wake up, you ask yourself how you want to live your day. That *"How* do I want to live?" speaks to an intentional expression of self, a chosen opportunity.

Throughout the day you think about it, carrying with you your idea of how to live. Once you get to the end of the day, you ask yourself, *Well, how did I do?* This makes you conscious of the narrative you are creating, making it harder to fall into automatic pilot. As you begin becoming conscious of the self you're carrying through a day, you can begin seeing the possibilities of the self you might carry in your tomorrows. You can begin making adjustments to obtain better fidelity to yourself. Musicians do this, learning to adjust finger positions and mouth positions and breath support to produce a clearer, truer voice and tone.

Seneca's suggestion is one means to get feedback on alternative measures of self that are larger than a business. Starting a day by deciding how you want to live, going inward to that spacious room of yourself to get away from external influence to create your intention—it opens the door for you to emerge. From there, you can go out into the world, relate, interact, and do your best work. Intention provides a mission to express yourself as the vehicle of your own life.

Set the intention to live that way and then give yourself space to express it, realigning with yourself as you move through your day. If you're doing that, carrying that sense of self all day, then you're probably also living a truer version of yourself. Over time, as you do that, life becomes smoother. You'll likely have fewer energy leakages because you're in flow. Things just move the way they should. You begin to see yourself again, to feel yourself again, to reappear in your own life.

Contrast that with a starting point where you literally just jump into your email inbox every morning, destabilizing your rested mind from the first minute you awake. From there, it's very hard to pull things back to yourself. If I wake up, immediately check my email, and half an hour later, sit down and meditate, I could probably bring back some calm and space. That's risky, though, because if one of those emails were particularly undesirable, it might hook itself into my whole day. Better to start by expressing the self's strong conviction of what is important and what you want or intend to achieve. That's a much better way of filling out a to-do list. It will help you filter out the unimportant and allow space for you.

RETURN ON ME

I've mentioned getting a return on yourself as one measure of a life-profitable business. A life-profitable business will help you get that return by giving you the means to be present in your most meaningful experiences every day. Why is this so important? It gives you continuing intimate knowledge of your single most important asset: yourself.

Just before I exited WooThemes, I was introduced to a financial adviser—that's his professional skillset, at least. Our initial introduction was around helping me think through my next stage: if I were to exit WooThemes, what would the financial conservation look like?

Whilst we were still getting to know each other, he told me about how he bought antique Ferraris for significant amounts of money, say, a quarter million dollars. Then he would renovate, restore, improve, and sell them for almost double. I was flabbergasted because, I mean, it was a ridiculous amount of money for an old car, even if it was a Ferrari, and it seemed extremely risky to me. So I asked him, "Isn't this an incredibly risky investment? Isn't this an incredibly risky business to run, especially since it's obviously not your primary business?"

And he said, "Adii, you know what? You could ultimately invest in any asset class. Doesn't matter how exotic it seems to the outside. The only condition is that you know that asset class intimately."

He specifically used that word, *intimately*. He went on to explain that he knows exactly what the market wants, what a vintage Ferrari buyer is looking for, and how much the vehicles that he purchases are worth. Because he knows all those things and continues to cultivate that intimate knowledge of vintage Ferraris, he is in a position to profit from that pursuit and practice more often than he would actually lose money.

Again, you can invest in any asset class, no matter how exotic it may seem from the outside, and you can get a return as long as you know it intimately.

You are an asset.

If we each consider ourselves—our true and developed selves—an asset, we are uniquely positioned to get a return. Nobody else can be as intimate with this asset as we, ourselves, can be. There is a case to be made, then, that one of the better assets, if not the best asset, in which you can invest is yourself. It doesn't matter how exotic that may seem. We become intimate by consistently caring for ourselves, by making sure that we are in alignment ourselves, by creating a space for ourselves to develop and bear fruit.

You may feel that any time away from the business cannot be justified because you do not think about yourself as your most important asset, the asset where you have the best insider opportunity to make gains. That has happened because you have substituted a business identity for your true identity. Investing in yourself, though, means you gain access to more of yourself, which you can then bring to bear for your business. When we look after ourselves, of course we function as better entrepreneurs. And, like the financial adviser, you are not limited to a lone entrepreneurial pursuit. You can be the entrepreneur of your business *and* of yourself.

I have found that when I'm a better human being, I act as a better human being in my relationships. And when I'm a better person in those relationships, those relationships become nodes of significance, increasing my sense of a meaningful, rich life. And when I look after my mental health at work and create the space for myself to do other things, I can pursue and succeed at ambitious personal goals, such as running a marathon in less than four hours. Then there's a return on that, too, because I now have that medal and the memory that I actually did it. It is a resource to draw upon, this experience of knowing I can tackle and succeed at something difficult for anyone. That self-knowledge changes the context of every challenge I will face for the rest of my life. And I can relay the lessons I learned there to my children.

In economics we have the concept of the efficient-markets hypothesis, simplified as "No single person can outperform the market in the long term." Our concept of "return on me" debunks that notion because you're literally just focusing on yourself. Because you know this asset class so intimately, you can continue investing in this asset appropriately and outperform the marketplace forever, mostly because this marketplace is a marketplace of one, which is you.

Nobody can do you better than you, and whatever you have to give to the world can only come from you.

Knowing that you can always grow is a version of freedom that probably resonates with all entrepreneurs. If an entrepreneur started a business today and they had to pitch investors for money, they'd probably include a quantifiable metric about the size of the opportunity, often total addressable market. They'd say, "The market size is $10 million, and I think I can capture 10 percent of it." That already imposes a limit, and you probably can't get beyond that. In self-growth there is no limit. It's the ultimate freedom to know that, for as long as I desire, I can walk down this path of investing in myself and gravitating toward things I absolutely love as an entrepreneur of self and of business.

I'm always going to be an entrepreneur. Perhaps you always will be too, driven by a desire for freedom and creating things—manifesting parts of yourself "out there." It's self-invention and self-expression at the same time.

Given this, the biggest opportunity for changes leading to life profits is found within you. That's where you have the most power. That's where you have the most control. That's where you'll see the biggest returns. As you realize those returns, your fruition ripples out into the worlds of others. We'll talk about the importance of that in the next chapter.

REFLECTION

"Each man must look to himself to teach him the meaning of life. It is not something discovered: it is something molded."
—Antoine de Saint-Exupéry

Where are you compromising your life? Where are you sacrificing your values, your meaning? How have the opinions, esteem, and feared judgment of others affected how you do business, how much you do business, and what you're trying to achieve? What might be your highest pursuits according to your values, instead, and would those who applaud you for them be the same people who applaud your business? What are you doing when you feel the most at peace, the most self-respect, the greatest sense of being yourself? How much do those shape your life?

CHAPTER FIVE

LIFE-PROFITABLE VALUES

THE PRIORITY OF OTHERS

> *We who lived in concentration camps*
> *can remember the men who walked*
> *through the huts comforting others,*
> *giving away their last piece of bread.*
> —Viktor Frankl, *Man's Search for Meaning*

I t's a triumph of the human self, choosing the integrity of one's own values no matter the situation. As humans, one of our deep-seated values is valuing others. It's intrinsic, this drive to be part of the shape of others' lives and have them be part of the shape of ours.

Valuing others as a value in itself is first a recognition that everyone else also yearns and deserves to live out their fullest selves. And it is a recognition that everything each of us does ripples out to the others in our lives for good or for bad. Our expressions of self don't stay contained and bounded without repercussions in the wider world. The self is of the world. You, me, all of us—we are in it together.

It is in our nature to connect and to belong, to find joy and meaning in our shared lives and experiences. It's so integral to who we are and what we are that love and belonging precede self-actualization on Abraham Maslow's hierarchy, a depiction of humankind's universal needs. Others help us fulfill our impulse to seek wholeness. Connection is part of how we express our fullest and truest selves.

Your life-profitable business also needs others to fulfill itself. Naturally, if those others are thriving and growing, intent on living out their best selves to the best of their ability—naturally, what they contribute to your business's success will always be better than if they were stagnating or even languishing. That means that a life-profitable business cannot only be concerned with people performing functions; it must be concerned with functioning people performing. People function better when they evolve in a larger context of a whole and well-lived life. Life-profitable businesses make room for that larger life instead of crowding it out. And where they can they facilitate—even invest—in others' journeys of growth and meaning, they do so.

No one you hire can ever be as invested in the business as you, the owner. But everyone is fully invested in themselves and their lives, with a version of a life they long to live. If they can't live that, it eventually impacts their work as well. A life-profitable business gives employees room to build that life, which, in turn, impacts their work. Setting up your business in a way that allows people to grow, to self-actualize, to be fruitful in meaningful ways while doing the collective work of the business will probably mean a productive business that gets better financial results.

THE RIGHT PEOPLE DOING THE RIGHT THINGS

So, if a life-profitable business cannot merely put people in roles to perform certain functions irrespective of who they truly are, how do we populate our teams?

Ultimately, we want to build the kind of team where we all agree that, as a collective, we work toward the same goal, while, as individuals, we each do stimulating, challenging, fun work. We want people not only suited to what they do but also suited to our particular business. Instead of hiring for skills, we hire for the right people, those whose values align with ours.

Alignment is key. Just as a car with wheels out of alignment makes steering harder, not to mention causing an uncomfortable ride, the vehicle of your business is helped or hindered by the positioning of those involved. Everyone must be moving in the same direction, working together to carry things forward.

Looking at others who could or already work at your business, you must ask yourself if the business is a good fit for the person and in keeping with who they are right now. Will it serve them as an individual? And is the person a good fit for the business and the others already there? For instance, do they have a quality like maturity or leadership or extroversion or empathy—a quality the team and business need?

Misalignment means friction where the business meets the individual, and friction can be catastrophic. Like tectonic plates converging, one must sink under the other, energy growing until it lets loose an earthquake with a tsunami of consequences rushing out. It's traumatic, probably with collateral damage, and that collateral damage can break down other structures that were otherwise healthy.

We ourselves create this friction when we ignore alignment between the world of the individual and the world of the business. If we don't hire for people whose interests and values align and overlap with the business, who can share the vision and goals, who are served by being part of the common effort, who serve the others involved too, eventually a team member feels so out of sorts in their own skin at work that the only way to rectify the misfit is to shed it altogether. Just slough off the business in search of something less wrong. The employee suffers, but the churn hurts the business as well.

It's better to intend to "do business with people who believe what you believe," as Simon Sinek says in *Start with Why*. It's important to have people around us who bolster our values rather than dilute them. After all, others rub off on us, as we rub off on them. Everyone associated with your business influences it, especially those most involved in the day-to-day. Less dissonance in your business and life occurs with aligned groups of people.

People who share values can form a dynamic community as they get behind a shared mission. In fact, the shared values create the opportunity for something higher: a shared ethos. The Oxford dictionary, according to the online site Lexico, defines *ethos* as "The characteristic spirit of a culture, era, or community as manifested in its beliefs and aspirations." In the case of a life-profitable business, the aspiration is self-actualization for you and for those associated with the business.

The overlap of values for those in a business creates a community core. Our joint efforts can ripple outward and affect the world around us instead of creating choppiness. It's important to remember that there is life at play here.

People will grow away from a shared belief as they or their priorities change. We can support them as they do this, through a shared spirit of transparency. We let ourselves know one another, which dynamically lets us understand what is happening and what should happen.

DIVERSITY

A shared value system doesn't mean homogenization and exclusion. If life-profitable businesses value the self-actualizing individual "other," by definition we end up with a diverse group. We want this inclusion of diverse viewpoints and experiences, to prevent building an echo chamber. Echo chambers have a paucity of ideas, something to be rejected by entrepreneurs. Whether diversity happens through gender or race or heritage or life experience, diverse teams will always outperform teams that are homogenous—a simple online search will back me up.

What's interesting is the notion that, if we're all equal based on the fact that we have equal opportunities to pursue ourselves, then our differences fail to matter anymore because we're essentially acknowledging that since we are different, we should explore those differences. We're not a threat to one another, because we're pursuing our own selves. Nobody else is going to be doing that better than you. You and I working together is not a zero-sum game.

We can both win when the ultimate goal is not me getting promoted over you or me taking something of yours or me forgetting that your self-interest must be served alongside mine—we both win by simply pursuing the best versions of ourselves out in the open, helping one another where our interests overlap.

Diversity of experience brings more wisdom to your team, and as the leader, you can draw on that. I used to think that, as the leader, I had to make all the decisions, and they had to be great. I was the one who had to fix everything. But, of course, that was conditioning, the toxic masculinity underlying the entrepreneurial archetype we've been yoked to.

I found out that leadership is not just me going off on this path and running as fast as I can and making decision, decision, decision, decision. My primary responsibility and yours is facilitating great decision making, and diversity and inclusion go a long way toward that. This relieved a great deal of anxiety for me. I don't know all the answers, so how can I have all the answers?

Of course, as the owner, the final decision is yours—you can't abdicate responsibility. But with everyone collectively committed to the enterprise for real reasons of their own, you can ask the community to figure it out together. You'll have so much more breadth and depth of viewpoints with a team chosen with an eye toward inclusiveness and value alignment.

In my much-improved way of making decisions, the decision itself is not my focus. The process of making the decision is. It's sometimes difficult to execute and listen to diverse opinions. But I've found it's worth it, especially on the bigger decisions or challenges or questions that we've had. I've often told my team, "Let's have a rigorous debate about this." Being transparent and inclusive and facilitating these conversations and decisions doesn't make it a democracy. But everyone has a voice, and if you take the opportunity to bring value to the conversation by letting people share their opinions and ideas and the reasons for them, you and the whole team are much better informed.

When individuals have that opportunity to be involved in those conversations, they take more responsibility for their opinions as well. You're likely going to get quality input and prevent or lessen risk. Decisions are always on a spectrum. There are probably one or two wrong decisions, and there might be an absolute best decision. But as long as you're making a good-ish decision, you're probably okay.

So again, it doesn't have to be the perfect decision. It just needs to not be the fatal decision. Having that diversity in the room when making decisions probably means you're getting further away from the fatal decision and closer to the hypothetical perfect decision.

There are a couple other ways to think of diversification in relation to your business. I think just about everyone has heard the statement "You are the average of the five people you are around the most." For something like character and value alignment, you'd want none of those five to drop the average for the rest. Your group will have a better chance of making a more impactful difference in whatever direction you move together.

For the same reasons, the first members of your team, your core group, should share an entrepreneurial sensibility. They can bring different skills to the mix but should be able to understand what it is to take risk, innovate, and create value in the world. In other words, look out for those who, like you, show signs of being entrepreneurs of the self. If they've been doing that, they'll be able to, first of all, understand the concept of life profitability. But second, if your first community members possess and express something of the entrepreneurial mindset, they'll add a lot of strength to the characteristics needed to push a startup forward. Your core team will be your most prominent community members, and they'll drive a lot of action. Hiring for entrepreneurial talent coupled with a healthy sense of life's importance will help ensure the action drives forward in the right directions.

But, of course, as a life-facing business, we ought not to limit our group of five (or seven or ten) to those directly operating in the sphere of your business. Who is it you want to be in the small group influencing your behavior, shaping who and what you are?

I told you about how my wife, Jeanne, was involved within the greater realm of the business, though not working within the business itself. And then I had my best friend, De Wet, whose realms included both my business and our overlapping personal lives. My attention turns toward these two a lot, so they are, without a doubt, two people who factor into my average. And they should be.

Who are you spending the most attention on? If you have a look at the five people with whom you spend the most time or energy, you partly answer the question of for whom you've been optimizing your entrepreneurial journey. You've been putting them in the first ring of others. Are they appropriate to who you are and your values?

For example, if the five people start with my banker, my lender, and my shareholders, it's very obvious that I'm putting their interests ahead of anyone else's. But if there's a mix here of spouse or significant other, kids, best friend, team members, and maybe also I'm volunteering at a local community project for the greater community—if these are a regular part of my life, there is a diversity in my life that speaks to a healthy ecosystem that sustains me and those with whom I interact and can affect. These intentionally chosen others definitely show for what and for whom I'm optimizing the outcome or the goals of my business.

Diversity in your life and in your workplace is an important life-profitable value.

LEAD YOUR COMMUNITY

I found a quote from marketing authority Seth Godin that says, "Begin by choosing people based on what they dream of, believe and want, not based on what they look like. In other words, use psychographics, instead of demographics." The psychographics to start with are your own. Remember that you start with the self and take self-expressive action that drops in the waters of the world. That forms the first inner concentric ring in a model of how to prioritize and understand your interactions and impact in the world. As your effect moves out, it creates the next circle, that of others, and from there ripples to your business, which operates in the larger arenas of your town, country, world.

This means that considerations of others as relates to your business start with you: you lead with your values, your ethos. You look for other people with similar beliefs and aspirations, no matter their demographics. They don't have to be 100 percent the same. But there should be some healthy overlap that creates a bond. The bond deepens as your community within the business begins to share experiences based on shared meaning.

Each person brings meaning to the mix that is shared by the group. In the chapter's initial quote, the men who shared bread brought their own meaning into a terrible darkness. That shone a light: by their sacrifice of food, they acknowledged the importance of others and connectedness and group. Even in the context of a concentration camp, you had human beings expressing a desire to belong to the community, even though it was a community that they were forced into, by connecting in the most human way possible, which was literally sharing bread. Love and belonging are part of a process of self-actualization. Selflessness does not empty itself; it fills with selfhood.

This innate need for belonging is a critical component in considerations of the others around you. You have it; your team has it. Expressing it benefits all. And there's a reciprocity at work: if you share, you express your humanity and realize it. And if you allow yourself to receive, you acknowledge that you must connect with others; you can't be self-sufficient. In light of the human need to belong and connect, receiving, too, then, is an act of self-actualization. This reciprocity of giving and receiving according to the diverse gifts your team has makes for sustainability, an important characteristic of life-profitable businesses.

Sharing takes trust, of course, and vulnerability and openness. Your business—you—must possess these qualities and support them in team members. It means breaking down some of the barriers between life and work. Instead of only talking about work, you shift to talking about people's larger lives. That immediately lets people get to know one another in a context of reality. And that lets team members make adjustments organically with greater insight and more realistic expectations of others. It lets you, as the leader, take note of an employee who is not doubling down on self-investment. If a salaried employee is clocking sixty hours, you can work together to figure out why. Why is work taking so long? Has something happened in the work environment to create distraction? Is something going on with their health or at home? Are they escaping from the rest of their life? Together you can make adjustments that let that employee get back to your shared interest: promoting the best interests of each and all.

Goodwill goes a long way.

Acknowledging work in the context of others' lives doesn't mean a collapse of boundaries, though. In a work situation where people are open and expressive, it's easy to begin to think of your work community as a family. That's a mistake. I get why entrepreneurs fall into this. I don't think there's a malicious intent in saying "We're all family here" and the like, but we only have one family. To place work colleagues on the same pedestal as your real family minimizes your family's importance. And if you're saying this to employees, you're minimizing their families and elevating your importance. It might begin to make you think that your business should be as important to them as it is to you. That puts them in an unfair position.

Remember that work is not an expansion of your family. It's an overlap of shared interests, a shared goal, this business pursuit that we share. And it's only for right now. Just as for you, meaning-making experiences for employees usually don't happen at work. They occur in the deepest and most enduring parts of life. Meaning lives in births, deaths, triumphs a long time in coming, self-mastery, the pursued passions that make us thirst and sweat. Your business cannot compete with those, nor should it. What it can do is welcome those who are busy living all that out. What it can do is respect it, enable it, and rejoice that such people are willing to bring all that to bear for your business right now.

SPACE

It's a vain exhortation to say leave your personal life at the door or leave work at work. People flow into different contexts, shaped by what's come before, what's coming now, and what they expect to come later. We feel and respond to the world around us, experiencing life as a continuum. A great day at work comes home. So does a bad day, even if we take the time to process it or maneuver around it to function properly in our new context. A great start to the day goes to work with us, providing momentum. Something like a motor accident, even a minor one, will affect the workday in the other direction.

All this creates a sort of energy moving in all directions from our work experiences. For me, it might ripple out to my wife and my kids. For someone else on the team, it might affect an elderly parent. Or friends who function as a family group.

And herein lies an opportunity for us as entrepreneurs: knowing there's an energy that travels out into the world of others, we can make it one of light, of warmth, and of growth. At the shared core of our business activities, we can fan an ember that we intend to be a force for good. We can do it purposely and purposefully because it behooves a life-profitable business to acknowledge we're dealing with humans and human lives.

First, then, the workplace culture needs to be one that takes responsibility for the ripples our business will have in the lives of those it interacts with. And not just them— each person your business affects will touch others, who will touch still others, and so on. People need the elbow room to be human and be treated in a way that jives with that reality.

That means giving others space for their larger lives, lived with self at the center. "Self first" is the watch phrase for each of them. Life-profitable businesses cannot allow team members to become servants of or sacrifices to your overfed entrepreneurial dragon, feeding it time and energy that belongs to others. We know from bitter experience that doing that only leaves a person hollow and eventually unable to give any more. We don't want people burnt to a crisp. We want fleshy, well-nourished people whose self-investment makes them committed to business activities as part of their thriving.

Space to live looks different to different people. That's why having open communication in a life-first context with employees is so important. If life is self-expression, you'll find some of your employees want the space to grow professionally, learning new skills and getting a chance to move laterally or up. On the other hand, I had an assistant in my previous business, called Dominique, who wasn't interested in that.

Dominique was so, so good in her role. Naturally, I felt ambitious for her, wondering how I could make space for her to advance. Eventually, it got to a point where I said, "Dom, I mean, I can increase your salary every year with inflation and a little bit of extra. But what does your career path here look like? What do you want to learn? What do you want to do? What do you want to do to kind of—I want to pay you more money."

She said, "I'm just really happy doing this work. I really enjoy it. There's nothing at this stage that I feel I need to learn."

For Dom, who enjoyed her work, why would she devote space in her life toward ascending the ladder? She probably decided, "Work-wise, this is perfect for me," and evolved in many other life aspects that made more sense for her.

Dom was a rock star, that person who truly makes up the foundation of your business. They're happy with the work they're doing at this stage. They show up and do the work every single day because that's what they love. Every business needs those people, just as they need those who are in a place where they want to ambitiously explore. For us, the entrepreneurs, the point is to enable others to live the lives they want to live, not just as an act of altruism, but of self-preservation. We must provide the right ground for things to take root.

It can be scary to promote and fuel others' ambition as an entrepreneur, and you may not want to give your employees space for their growth, let alone invest in it. They might leave, you worry.

But thinking this way puts you into a scarcity mindset. Building from your own values of self, collecting others who share those values, all of you agreeing to perform at your best for self-expression and self-actualization— these set a standard and a context. If someone shifts to different priorities, if someone outgrows their role so staying would mean stagnation, you've got to release them. They must move along to continue on their life-first path. And we and our team do the same, welcoming someone else who is at the right place to share our work and values.

I had an engineer who did not join us in making the transition from Conversio to the company that bought us out. The reason was not because he was mad at me or anyone else. He just decided it was time for him to be an entrepreneur and founder, and he wanted to work on his own software startup.

What a beautiful thing. I think about that—me being a stepping-stone for someone. This engineer helped me build my company, and now he was rippling out, having his own impact in the world. I'm proud of that.

In this case, the engineer was proactive and honest, which meant we could find a way to transition him out. There was proper handover. When you honor someone else to say, "I trust you enough for you to be your whole self, both at work and in life," that person, knowing you are trustworthy, has little reason to act in a malicious, detrimental way, for instance, suddenly one day not showing up for work.

It's better to acknowledge that, as an entrepreneur, relationships in our sphere aren't built for forever most of the time. It's best for all parties to be up-front and just be honest and transparent about it. When we're all just doubling down on ourselves, like we agreed on in the beginning of our associations, it's implied that, eventually, our paths might diverge. But we're still doing the same thing as in the beginning. We still have the exact same shared interest, which was and is the space to be ourselves.

Mutual respect and trust, letting go of white-knuckle control, and taking pride in your influence—these inform the ring of "other." We all need others, and your business needs them too.

IMPACT IN THE WORLD

I had wanted to engage in social entrepreneurship at the beginning of Conversio's journey, but back then I was still thinking sequentially: I needed a certain amount of commercial success to come first in order to do things that were more experimental, more charitable in nature. It was at that stage that I realized there was another way besides the sequential to think about business, setting the stage for life profitability. I thought, *How can I build a business in a way that serves me and my first circle, which is my family?*

Doing that would mean focusing on a healthy self and thinking about what I'd take back to my family once I finished work for the day. I thought, *What version of Adii do they get after a tough day's work or a tough week's work or sometimes a tough quarter's work? And, yes, what is the financial consideration in that? Can I use the fruits of my labor as a way to reinvest in my entire life?* And that was at my first circle.

And I drew a second circle around the first, the circle of others. I thought, *Okay, if I have a dozen or so new people on my team, is there a way in which I can help them to do a similar thing for their families?* I wanted them to also be able to say, "I can work and produce and be involved with this community called Adii's business in a way that first serves my family. I could show up as the best version of myself, and I can take these fruits of my labor and reinvest them at home."

This resulted in the life-first culture summed up in our first culture document. It declared, "We want to do challenging, stimulating, valuable work, but the most meaningful experiences we can have in our lives are outside of work and outside of business."

We felt this approach could do exponential good in the world: if I was able to serve my family—to promote well-being as our foundation—and this enabled just one family member to do even one charitable, philanthropic deed, what had started at the business as life profits would carry out into the world for good. If everyone on my team did the same thing, perhaps inspiring their spouse or a sister or a friend—if we enabled good acts by making room for people to live larger lives—then this thing would become exponential. Here was the genesis of that notion of concentric circles constantly rippling outward, overlapping and amplifying from many selves.

Everyone sits at the center of their own concentric set of circles, and all of us have the same needs. On Maslow's hierarchy, there's a need for basic survival, for safety and security, for love and belonging, for accomplishment and recognition, and for self-actualization. Ask yourself what opportunities you give your employees to meet these needs. If you let employees show up as their entire selves at work, if you give them ways to self-actualize, to accomplish, to belong to a community that recognizes them, they are likely to stay longer than they normally would, and you will have created legacy.

Legacy is that ambition that ultimately lives on beyond your human life. It grows from the decisions and actions we take today and every day. They reverberate in time and in space, legacy growing with each ripple. Remember the men sharing comfort and bread in concentration camps; their legacy lives on, inspiring still. Legacy, or the lack of it, is your destiny after you're gone.

In the next chapter, we'll start remodeling your destiny by shaping your actions in the realm of others.

REFLECTION

"We who lived in concentration camps can remember the men who walked through the huts comforting others, giving away their last piece of bread. They may have been few in number, but they offer sufficient proof that everything can be taken from a man but one thing: the last of the human freedoms—to choose one's attitude in any given set of circumstances, to choose one's own way."
—Viktor Frankl, *Man's Search for Meaning*

How could choosing your own way, no matter the hardships you face in life and business, enable you to better nourish others? Where would the meaning in that be for you? How would nourishing others in these ways nourish yourself? How would this depart from what you're doing now?

CHAPTER SIX

MODELS OF LIVING PROFITABLY

OTHERS

*Ubuntu is very difficult to render in a Western
language. It speaks of the very essence of being human.
It is to say, "My humanity is caught up, is inextricably
bound up, in yours." We belong in a bundle of life. We
say, "A person is a person through other persons." It
is not, "I think therefore I am." It says rather, "I am
human because I belong. I participate. I share."*

—Reverend Desmond Tutu

A life-profitable business does not need human capital, pawns to move around from function to function. A life-profitable business needs three-dimensional people, whole people offering their abilities freely. We can't predict all the abilities and talents the people we hire possess. If they show up to work as their truest selves, and we give them room to be themselves, their gifts will emerge over time, ingredients that come together in magical and unexpected ways that benefit your business and those within it. Expressing more of ourselves ends up, then, creating space and magic that empowers the pursuit of meaningful experiences at work. The real meaning, though, occurs in the ripples beyond the work. We can amplify those ripples by strengthening the core from which they emanate: people.

EXPLORATION

Money Isn't Everything

Flexible work, remote work, holiday time, a sense of community, not putting undue deadline pressure on team members—these things hold worth for people who value being people and not just cogs. My team showed me that meaningful, stimulating work along with the way they were able to work was more important than money alone. Over the years, some team members had better financial offers, but stayed with us anyway. This is good news for smaller concerns. You cannot compete with the largest players out there in terms of remuneration, no matter how much you wish you could. Those aligned with your company's values, who see an opportunity to find a work community that suits them, will join you anyway. I'm not suggesting you can give someone an awesome work environment and then underpay them. But when you're competing, not just based on what you can afford in the labor market but on many other factors, it does change the equation. There are enough people in the labor market for whom life first is important. They will happily consider your offer.

Where would you like to work? Beyond a particular industry, company, and rate of pay, you'd like to work in a place and space where you are comfortable, where you have conditions enabling your best work and supporting you when you fall into a slump. Everyone feels the same way. And why shouldn't they have it that way? If it's better for them, it's also better for the business.

Individuals have different "best" environment needs. Some need noise, others quiet. Some like clutter, others spare lines and nothing out of place. This being the case, one way to provide individualized workplaces is through remote and distributed companies and teams. It's not possible for every company, of course. But whatever your situation, be flexible enough to help employees create workspaces that enable them to figure out what makes sense in terms of how they work, and what and whom they need around them to do their best.

And we must encourage the kind of inclusivity and openness that lets a team member talk about something that isn't working. Remote workers sometimes report loneliness, for instance, and may need strategies to navigate that. Only a conversation can give us the opportunity to improve a situation that detracts from a person's ability to bring their best self to work and to live as themselves.

It's draining to not be yourself, to constantly have to filter, adjusting who you are. It's draining to interact based on rules that you might not agree with or fully understand. The path of least resistance is for all of us just to stay true to ourselves. When we stay close to our cores in that sense, we stay close to our natures. There's no additional energy that we have to expend to interact and move through our lives and through our days. We're not constricted. When you have the space to be more of yourself, you feel more positive, more energized, and happier to take on the challenges that are ahead of you that day.

People enjoying that in your workplace will contribute more to your community, and the members will tend toward forming a culture. If you've been hiring for values and diversity, you've gone a fair way in shaping the culture of your company. But you've got to go further.

A Human Workplace Culture

My friend and mentor Jason Cohen, said, "Culture happens to you whether you do something about it or not." If you want to create a workplace that empowers human beings at their best, you must create a culture to that end.

It takes a conscious effort and consideration. If you don't, a culture develops anyway, and it may not support the employees and the company in the way you'd hope.

Culture is merely a way to codify the things that people do. You can either be proactive about that, constantly influencing, feeding, and nurturing it, or you can allow people to run riot. Then you lose the opportunity to shape the narrative. If that happens, you'll likely get to a point where the vocal minority, in a good or bad sense, will be the ones telling the story about your culture, your team, and your company. You've not given them a central point of a shared narrative around what your culture is, what your values are, and what that actually means to all of you on a daily basis.

The biggest part of culture are the values we all agree to uphold. The values will always first come from the founder and/or the founding team. It starts with that first ring of the self, the core. The culture is next influenced by the team members that come after the core is formed, those team members you choose for shared values and for the uniqueness they can bring to the team. It ultimately comes down to taking these shared values and putting them together into some kind of remix that makes sense for the company.

At Conversio, we formally created a culture code. That being said, cultures are living things, not something carved in stone. It's important to intend to create a living, growing document. At first, it was just me writing out culture code statements. I hadn't even hired any team members yet. It's remarkable that when I dug them up years later, I discovered how relevant they still are, reflecting some of my true core values.

Here's what I came up with:

1. Our core passion is to create value for our customers.
2. As individuals we work on things that we're passionate about and things that challenge us. If these aren't present, we'd rather seek alternative opportunities.
3. Our team is only as strong as the weakest link. As such, I will take care of myself first and ensure that I can provide my best to the customers, the team, and the company.
4. Every customer deserves a fair opportunity to receive and experience the outcome they desire.
5. We are what we do, not who or what we say we are. (Actions speak louder than words.)
6. I will be transparent and honest even when it hurts.
7. Relationships are important inside and outside of the company.
8. We value great experiences for ourselves and our customers.
9. We strive to learn something new every day.

10. We aim to be as efficient as we can in everything we undertake.

Values

Eventually, over time, we distilled this to five values and two statements. It's important to really narrow down to the most important of your initial list because you must live values if they are to have any meaning. They are things you aspire to, explaining how you are working today, who you are today, and who you want to be going forward. For instance, at Conversio, the five values that emerged after distillation were (1) honesty, (2) rebellion, (3) passion, (4) independence, and (5) curiosity.

Most of these are understandable. Rebellion, for us, dealt directly with moving toward a life-first, therefore life-profitable business. We were willing to go our way, disrupt the business status quo, how or if we'd take on external funding, and change the way we worked and communicated. We wanted empathy to dominate our product. We wrote our statement on rebellion this way: "We are rebellious at heart; we aspire to be kind and responsible to our environment and society, while being an inspiration for others." We wanted rebelliousness to inspire constructive real-life action.

Think your values through as they would be applied in real life. It's easy to have a "value" such as "We value honesty." But what does that really mean? It needs much more context because nobody values dishonesty. Does valuing honesty mean we will tell the customer when we have screwed up and fully remunerate them for damages? Remember, culture is merely a way to codify the things that people *do*.

People need contextual guidance for a team to rally around an idea. They need to fully understand how that idea relates to them. Everyone understands at some kind of higher level why it's important to be honest or why it's important to be a learner or focus on improvement. But how those things are modeled can mean different things. By crystalizing cultural values contextually, bringing them into our particular space where we are today, we create awareness that can be applied in real life in real time. Otherwise, all our words are just dogma. Your value-based culture document should provide strong orientation when there is a question of right action. We want an alignment to living out our best according to our shared values. We bolster each other and are strong together.

PRACTICES

To value the selfhood of others is to provide them the opportunity to live truly, both inside and outside work. Each business will have particular ways they can best do that, but I've tried and had success with several methods that help achieve it.

Holiday Mode

If others are to have enough space to have meaningful experiences outside work, of course they need good time off. So often people are still connected to work through devices instead of disconnecting from business and connecting to their lives. No one can serve two gods. Certainly, I can't please my family if I'm working whilst on holiday or still tethered to work by phone. And certainly, I can't do my best work while distracted by my holiday. The same is true of team members.

When they were on holiday, as well as regular evenings and weekends, we encouraged our employees to switch off all notifications, so no email or Slack messages. We expected them to be offline. And we honored time off by not sending any kind of message unless it was of absolute urgency. Then we would probably phone and say, "Sally, you know we wouldn't bother you on your holiday if it weren't urgent. We're in such a difficult spot right now. We absolutely need you," which is sometimes the case on small teams. Sometimes there is just that specialist, the one person who can do something. But interruptions had to be a real emergency. Creating true space and expecting team members to live inside it, pursuing their lives without work encroaching on their inbox or their headspace—enforcing this value that life is first makes a difference to employees.

We all know those employers that give time off, but begrudgingly. We all know those employees who only use their vacation days when they're going to expire or who use them as paid sick days, anxious that their boss won't see them as serious enough. It might even be a case of a company culture that tacitly expects employees to not take breaks. This is definitely not modeling the value of others.

Our team members understood that if they took a day, a week, or two weeks off, they didn't need to feel anxious. No one was going to be angry or resentful. No one was going to shout at them for not being around when something went wrong. When this is the norm, team members mutually support each other in taking space. The practice becomes a robust part of the culture, a process that everyone buys into. And the more it happens, the more entrenched it becomes. Being able to take time off and trusting team-mates enough to steady the ship whilst they're not there totally decreases that mental load, which is crucial. I, too, made a conscious choice to not be the only one capable of carrying out certain business aspects. I had to model what I expected from employees.

We tried different approaches to encouraging team members to actually take time off and to do it regularly. First, we had unlimited holiday. If you had completed amazing work in four days by bringing your whole, true self, by all means take a long weekend every week. The only proviso was to take teammates into account, structuring your time off around them if they needed you. You just needed "approval" from a related team member to have your back, meaning redundancy. So, an engineer on the team would basically need to have approval from someone else on the engineering team for long amounts of time off. The others would be ready to step in when needed. The system created a good balance between self and others.

We discovered that employees felt guilty about taking time off, though. We eventually landed on a minimum holiday policy, which essentially required everyone on the team to take twenty-eight days off in any twelve-month window. Of those twenty-eight days, at least seven had to be consecutive days. It's great to take one or two days here or there, just do a quick little recharge, but sometimes we need a bigger reset.

Short notice was absolutely fine. If you needed to take the day off tomorrow, that was totally fine. It didn't require massive advance notice. We didn't even bother about half days. If you're taking a half day off or an extended lunch, it wasn't even necessary to book time off. Here we recognize that, most of the time, people need time off to live their normal lives, going to the doctor or visiting the hardware store across town that's only open during the week or whatever the case is.

We didn't police our policy. It didn't have a punitive quality but was instead encouraged and reinforced by everyone. If someone said, "Oh, I'm feeling pretty tired this week," team members would call out that person.

They would say, "You know what, Adii, hold on. When was the last time you took time off?" We all understood that the policy was in place to enable being your best self so you could do your best work.

Underlying this is a realization that the metric of hours worked is often moot. The reality is that smart, ambitious people are constantly thinking about work in any case. If they're performing, why sweat about the actual hours? If one of your team members needs to clear their head and go for a run during work hours (thinking about work, most likely), then it's ridiculous to expect them to make up that hour, especially when it enables them to come back clear-minded, possibly with a solution to something in mind.

Weekly Life Check-Ins

People being whole and true at work doesn't necessarily mean that interactions yield information that other team members might be interested in or even need to know. At Conversio, to prevent this, we used a software solution meant for work check-ins to share life plans, reasons for gratitude, and joys. Every Friday, a four-question prompt would arrive for each of us to fill out and submit:

- *How was your week?* We didn't qualify the question. It could be about work or not. People might talk about what work energized them or things that blocked their progress. But they talked about things outside work too. The best check-ins happened when an individual covered both work and the personal in their check-in. Those were more holistic.

- *What gave you the most joy this week?* Because we used a software solution for these Friday team check-ins, they were asynchronous and in written form. Still, you could always see that sparkle in someone's eyes, knowing they had the opportunity to share something about their life, about their kids, about them accomplishing something, about the new TV they bought. It was always such a fun answer set for each of us to read through. Most of the time, in our team at least, people shared their lives.

- *What are your weekend plans?* This was a very purposeful kind of prompt because no one in our team was expected to work on weekends. This question reinforced our support of life first. If we all shared our weekend plans, those things happening in life outside of work, it proved it was safe to care about your larger life and to live it out in the open. By asking this question, we renormalized the fact that our lives belong to us first and foremost. And we reinforced the notion that we expected everyone on the team to live first.

- *Does anyone on the team deserve a high five?* The idea was that we consciously gave credit where credit was due. In fast-paced team environments, it's easy for deserved acknowledgment, recognition, and validation to fall to the wayside. And sometimes someone will be doing something behind the scenes that no one really knows about. The acknowledgment let everyone know about great work and what made it great. And it let team members feel gratitude for a team member's effort, and a sense of pride. We were rooting for each other.

We also had a formal meeting every Wednesday, predominantly focused on work. It allowed us to sync up, know who was responsible for what project, and the top two or three things a team member was working on, which allowed everyone to feel a sense of orientation. But we always started off that meeting asking anyone to share a personal, a team, or just a company-wide win. And that could have been anything from, "Hey, my kid got third place yesterday in their dance competition!" to "Hey, we closed this deal and got a really big account!"

In both those practices, the Friday and Wednesday check-ins, we were aiming for the sense that we were working some number of hours per week, but for the rest of our time, there was a life out there that work did not eclipse. We reinforced that each of us was bigger than what we did on the job. These other things in our lives—they're significant; they're important. And they enable us to do our jobs in unique ways.

Team Retreats

Keeping in mind the primacy of family and personal relationships, strengthening a workplace community is not the same as trying to make everyone friends. As a distributed team working in far-flung places, it's not as if we could go out for drinks and become best friends anyway. But we could strive to develop an easy rapport, to be friendly, with work being our "in common." But no one had to feel as if they had to be friends, just friendly.

Because the team didn't get to have face time with one another, every seven or eight months, we created space in our work and personal lives to get together for a week and literally live together. We did two things in that week. First, we would spend about a quarter of our time having the bigger strategic discussions that are literally just easier to have around the same table and in person. I think anyone that's been on a Zoom call with ten-plus people knows how hard it is to really be inclusive and to have an efficient meeting where you're not speaking over each other.

For the rest of the time, we literally did the living together part. The idea was just for us to get to know each other. We were asking for each person to show up at these retreats as the person they were at home. So, the person that we don't get to see because we're not that close to each other, or the person who doesn't naturally appear within the work environment. And we promoted the idea that people share their passion.

For our group, at least, we shared a big fondness for food. On every retreat the thing that got planned first was not the work, but the food menu for the whole week. We literally had team members fly from all over the world to remote places, bringing things like electric mixers because there wouldn't be a mixer to bake a cake for someone's birthday. They would fly local ingredients into the country that we were visiting so that they could cook a very specific kind of recipe, maybe a recipe that they got from their grandma.

Our team member Stefano, nicknamed Papa Bear for his easy and perceptive understanding, is a hobbyist beer brewer. Every retreat, he brought us beer he brewed specifically for us to enjoy. A single meal together wouldn't move the needle toward friendly rapport. But presenting three different beers for a whole team and sharing that passion inspires others to do likewise. It becomes exciting to contribute and to share each other's passions.

We had a team member, Kim, who made Southern fried chicken. She hyped up this chicken for the longest time before the retreat. From her side, it took courage to cook a meal for twelve or thirteen people, especially after the buildup! And if I'm remembering correctly, this was her first retreat. For the team to see and appreciate her courage and to have an opportunity to have a meal that they would not have otherwise in their own home cultures creates a certain kind of familiarity, trust, and intimacy. There's something special and emotive around sharing food and drink made with care and enthusiasm because you declare, "We're not just going to grab some food, nourish our body, and go on to the next thing. We're actually going to dedicate this time and space for sitting together and sharing a meal."

I loved this because we weren't just sharing a meal. We shared a moment; we shared connection and intimacy. The culture of the team was strengthened by breaking bread. As we came from all over the world, for us it was a multicultural experience that in itself became part of our culture.

Self-Evaluation

Since Conversio had team members scattered on several different continents, team retreats presented an opportunity to conduct one-on-one, face-to-face employee evaluations. Unfortunately, that meant squeezing in all those private conversations in one week. This meant not only having two conversations per day at the height of our roster but also preparing for each of these. It was tiring in that week, and tired surely wasn't the way to have the best conversations, especially toward the end of the retreat.

We switched things up for the last two retreats we had before being acquired. We moved to employee self-evaluation, and that self-evaluation wasn't one-on-one, it was one-to-many because we did these in a group setting. I think the first time, we were literally sitting next to a pool. Some of us sat on beanbag chairs; others were just sitting on the ground, all sitting in a circle. There was no hierarchy. When it was your chance to speak, everyone turned to you instead of you walking to the center of an "audience." Everyone was still equal except for the fact that one person was speaking and setting the agenda. That was the only thing that separated them from the rest of the group in that moment.

The idea was for each person to take fifteen minutes to address their year. The other team members got fifteen minutes to interact, so a half-hour for each evaluation. I supplied eight basic questions that team members used as a guide to running their own self-evaluation. I got these questions from the online site KnowYourTeam, which asked its Watercooler members for the best asks for one-on-one meetings. The questions are:

1. How's life?
2. What are you worried about right now?
3. What rumors are you hearing that you think we should know about?
4. If you could be part of one accomplishment between now and the next retreat, what would it be?

5. What are your biggest time wasters?
6. Would you like more or less direction from the rest of us?
7. Would you like more or less feedback on your work? If more, what additional feedback would you like?
8. Are there any decisions you're hung up on?

Again, this was a guide, but each set their agenda, tone, context, and boundaries. The evaluations had the character of a debrief that informed us all. It wasn't limited to work; it was work as conducted in the context of a larger life. As individuals shared in this setting, the team enjoyed a sense of genuineness and intimacy. It had a profound effect on us.

I think everyone was concerned and nervous beforehand, but afterward everyone said, "This was really meaningful. We should continue doing this." Again, I think that proves the need for belonging and connection. When you give someone the opportunity to set their own agenda in terms of what they're sharing, you're also allowing them to illuminate or uncover certain things that aren't necessarily part of the natural flow of things within a work environment.

After the first of these self-evaluations, I asked everyone for feedback. Here's one response:

I...liked the range of emotion I experienced listening to everyone's stories, [and I was] caught by surprise every now and then. And it was a nice reminder that we really don't have the full picture of our closest people. They're experiencing this multilayered thing called life and there's really no way to separate that from work or vice versa. It was also a nice reminder of how privileged I am to be part of such a caring, empathetic team.

What a success in terms of a life-first business. This employee saw colleagues in the context of their humanity and shared in it. Their contextual human understanding can only benefit interactions with colleagues. With extra information relevant not only to work but to life, team members can flow around each other without as much friction.

There's also an opportunity for an enhanced sense of trustfulness and trustworthiness on the part of everyone involved. No one wants to let down others on a functional, performing team. And no one wants to be let down in a significant way. Charles Feltman, who wrote the book *The Thin Book of Trust: An Essential Primer for Building Trust at Work*, said, "The choice to trust consists of four distinct assessments about how someone is likely to act. These assessments are sincerity, reliability, competence, and care." (He notes that competence doesn't equal perfection and includes asking for needed help.)

For me, Feltman's list added up to me assessing whether I could trust everyone on my team to persistently and consistently show up as their whole self. If I could, it meant each practiced accountability. Accountability is better than any one measured result or lack of it. Accountability means willingness to improve, learn, and devote yourself to problems and find solutions. To my team it was "I am literally not going to measure and evaluate you; you're going to do that yourself. And I trust you enough to be able to do that and bring your whole self to even that conversation, as well." I chose each of these people for a reason; focusing on values and alignment meant each member practiced trustworthiness and trustfulness as part of a life-first workplace. This was evident in their self-evaluations.

EXPRESSIONS

In our check-ins and retreats, team members connected in genuine ways that gave everyone an idea of the contours of one another. This let them flow around each other more easily on the job. And I did so as well. By being more of myself at work, I broke down some boundaries, making myself more accessible. If my teammates did the same thing, then the connection, the bonds, the intimacy amongst all of us would be much greater. We belonged to something real—we were all citizens, members of this community, aspiring to this thing beyond oneself. And when we do that, we have those connections, we're most likely doing much better work as well because we're not just pulling in a similar direction to a stranger next to us. We're pulling in the same direction with someone and a few someones with whom we share that kind of bond, connection, and familiarity.

True teammates who are all joined in some exertion where you know each other's strengths and weaknesses, the places where each can help the other shine, creates a sense of mutual respect and compassion. That compassion has more gravitas than just "Hey, we're building this product in which we're both interested, and we have to do this because we have to pay the bills." It deepens the significance that we attach to this thing we've agreed to do together.

Naturally, it deepens our commitment too. And that inspires ownership.

Self-Expression through Leadership

Leaders don't have to be subject-matter experts to do a great job. In fact, expertise in one field or another doesn't mean a person also knows how to inspire others to a great outcome. At Conversio, we literally allowed anyone on the team to lead any project within the business. So, if it was a marketing project, it wasn't necessarily the marketer that had to lead it. An engineer could lead the marketing project if they felt passionate about it. Leading the project meant being responsible for having the right people in the room, virtually or otherwise, and to make sure that all stakeholder voices were represented.

They would keep me up to date, but ultimately, they were accountable to all of us. It didn't matter what the result was; the project leader had to communicate what was learned in the process, what we could possibly do next if we prioritized it, and what might be rectified or, if it worked out really well, what we could do to double down.

No one had to volunteer to lead a project, and some people never put their hand up. But for those who did, they didn't function as "temporary bosses" but instead as facilitators and coordinators. And we always left room in any project for the leader to figure out some of the deeper issues. The project brief was a strategic container, a sketch of what the final outcome needed to look like, and the leader painted the final portrait. We weren't handing someone a set of ten instructions and telling them to follow them to a T. That wouldn't give them ownership nor leave space for inspiration or taking the initiative. It wouldn't allow them to self-actualize if they were just running through a checklist. Anyone can do that. Instead, they could innovate and deliver something everyone could be excited about in the end.

There's a backstory to our successful "anyone can step up" project leader experiment. Around mid- to late-2018 we came out of a bit of a funk in terms of the cadence and pace at which we were releasing new things. We doubled down on greater accountability as we worked simultaneous multiple projects, calling it the eight-week rally. In this initiative, we publicly released and announced new software features every single week for eight weeks. We called it a rally because we wanted to rediscover that cadence of collaboration and ideation.

Because there were so many different things going on, it was impossible to have the same project leader for different projects in consecutive weeks. It would have probably meant overloading that person. The only way we were able to hit our "eight things in eight weeks" every single week was because we were very clear on the project leader and their team, creating transparency and peer-to-peer accountability. Individuals worked on multiple things simultaneously but had different leaders.

I think that everyone went into it with a bit of skepticism about how viable this push could be. But it ended up energizing people to put significant, meaningful things out into the world. I don't think we could have done such a push every second month, for instance, because it would have been tiring in the long run. As a short burst, though, our rally definitely served the purpose of reenergizing everyone and showing what results nonspecialist leaders could achieve.

There's satisfaction in being able to express skills and talents and abilities for the team, in being able to say, "I did it, and I did it for us," and then having the team feel appreciative. For people on your team who are themselves growing into entrepreneurs (of self), this is especially valuable. The opportunity to "apprentice" will keep them on your team longer. Employees today, especially young employees, migrate to other jobs at a higher rate than ever before. Companies need to fight for the right to keep the brightest employees. One way to do that is to help them express and develop abilities, expecting that eventually they will move on when it's their time. And that's appropriate. We each have our own life paths. We come together when our interests align, and when they diverge, we part.

One of my wildest dreams is the notion that individuals on teams of mine would eventually go on and found their own companies. I expressed this to my team often as a senior: "I would personally love for you to use this opportunity to learn from our journey, learn from me, and learn from each other; and if you ever step up to do your own thing, I would love to be a kind of advocate and promoter for that." Because I'm connected to these others, their successes enrich my life. I want to encourage entrepreneurial traits and abilities such as taking initiative, the ability to learn, and the ability to navigate uncertainty and the challenges that pop up. It's not that everyone decides entrepreneurship is for them, but coaching or prompting or prodding that enables growth can enrich many down the line. The ripples flow out into the world, in that we all share in creating meaning.

There will be, of course, people who are more reserved, introverts perhaps, who don't want to be center stage. It doesn't mean they cannot or do not express leadership on your team. Some of them may like to think first, talk later, and for that type of person, I would talk to them privately before a meeting if I think they actually could be the right person to head a project. I'd tell them why or encourage them to bring up an important point in the meeting that they had already shared with me.

And there are other ways people express leadership within your ranks. For instance, two well-respected members of my team were Stefano, who is Italian, and Maria, who is Spanish. English is a second language to them both, and neither was super-extroverted, yet they became known as Papa and Mama Bear. They are the oldest among us and brought diversity, preventing our core from crystalizing into a type A "bro" culture.

Stefano and Maria were not specifically tasked with leadership, but they took initiative nonetheless, in terms of communication and sharing wisdom. Both were very in tune with others' emotions; empathy was an easy thing for them to practice. When they spotted teammates or colleagues who seemed to be out of sorts in whatever way, they'd reach out. "Is something up?" they'd ask. "I noticed this. Am I misreading that?" When you provide a safe space at work, such things happen because coworkers are familiar, and they actually care for each other. It's important to notice and appreciate quiet leaders whose role on your team, quite without prompting, becomes to support others in bringing out their best.

There's another aspect to self-expression as leadership, one that pertains specifically to us, the owners. As I find ways for others to express more of their abilities—more of who they are—I, too, am expressing myself and also holding myself accountable. I'm accountable to my employees and the larger industry by the shared public nature of our digital lives. So are you. Anyone can go online to search a company's reputation. Online job sites allow employees to review employers. If you have created a workplace that creates and expresses consistent values, you will fare well compared to others.

Decision as an Expressive Process

Given that our values at Conversio oriented us toward right, life-first action, values had to, of course, be front of mind during decision making. Since all of us were aligned in our values, doing the right things for the right reasons, pushing forward together, we had to practice transparent decision making. Everyone needed to know and understand the context around decisions we were considering, along with the goals we had in mind.

We made the process inclusive and collaborative, in the sense that everyone in the workplace could contribute their thoughts and opinions. After all, what we did or didn't do would affect their lives. Team members who voiced opinions or concerns took responsibility for not just throwing a bomb or doing a mic drop. A person couldn't make the process more difficult for the decision maker, whether it was me or a project manager. Instead, if a team member spoke up, ideas needed to be nuanced and thought out, a piece of the puzzle that needed to come to light. And they needed to be something that actually could be implemented; otherwise they added little to the conversation.

And again, crucially, we linked all of this to our values. As a team, we were strong at creating a sense that our values were omnipresent. If there was an opportunity in a conversation, whether it was about marketing or sales tactical decisions or larger strategic issues, we used our values as the deciding factor. This was especially helpful when we came to a split in opinion. It sounds silly, but it might even be something minor, like "Should this website button be blue or green?"

We'd ask ourselves, "If we try to impose our values on this, what would those values advise us to do?" Initially, doing this felt very unnatural, but that changed with practice. Eventually, values would pop up organically when we had to make decisions or take action, because they had become so omnipresent. In the calm times, the easier times when conditions were favorable, we had agreed to these x many aspirational values. When the going got tough, we owed it to each other to hold fast to them. In the middle of a storm, what do our values mean? How do they help us chart the right course? Our values kept the rudder steady and the community strong and unwavering in uncertain times.

Values give us courage. They are a conscience that blows the horn for all to follow when decisions and actions are sobering. In the hardest times, shared and entrenched values keep us accountable.

The last thing to practice for collaborative, inclusive decision making is ensuring that when someone does take ownership of a project, they're given space to make decisions. After all, if someone is passionate enough to take on a project, they want to express something. They want the opportunity to run that project as they see fit and be responsible for it. There's enough space for team members to put their stamps down, knowing they must be accountable to the rest of the group. A person stepping up should not be afraid to make informed decisions or even to make judgment calls if available information and values don't make the decision self-evident.

Every decision has lessons as it plays out, which represent opportunities for the team. It's not about being right or wrong, or succeeding or failing. It's about saying, "This is what happened; this is what I learned. Here are things that we can try next." Essentially, you let the project manager plant the seeds for that conversation to continue, giving everyone else the starting point.

Space Revisited

The way we practiced work at Conversio gave our employees space in several ways. Of course, we gave them mental space. They didn't feel that sense, familiar to so many of us, that they had to check work emails in their nonwork time. We instead encouraged their time off. We didn't put undue performance pressures on employees, affecting stress levels not just at work, but during personal time. Employees also got time and space back by working remotely and skipping the commute. Neither did we chain employees to a set number of hours, instead focusing on performance and completion regardless of how long work tasks did or didn't take. We did all this because life needs space, headspace, energy, and time, along with the opportunity to move about in our own worlds. Being life-first for an individual means personal development and evolution. The collective should support that.

In the last chapter, I told you about one of my team members who chose not to move with us after the acquisition, instead setting off in a new direction to found his own software startup. It felt fantastic. He'd had the space to learn entrepreneurship "on the job" as we built Conversio. But he also had space to make the decision to set forth on his own journey. He knew he would not be judged in a negative, detrimental way. In fact, we were saying, "Yes, we fully support you. This is actually amazing. We're so happy for you!"

A couple of months after the acquisition, another employee told me she had some "unfortunate news": she was leaving us in about two months' time. The way we worked, she said, had created enough space in her personal life that she could take preliminary courses that allowed her to apply to medical school—and she had been accepted.

It turned out that in the previous year, she'd had a death in the family that made her question the decisions she had made. Thinking it over had reignited her original desire, a dream to be a medical professional. I felt so gratified that she actually used the word *space*. The space for her to be life-first meant she could take those first couple of educational steps, using us as a springboard into something completely different.

If we were not a life-first business, uninterested in creating life-profits, she wouldn't have had that same space to live as herself. At another, more traditional outfit, she would have been lashed to a forty-, fifty-, or even sixty-hour week. But great work isn't defined by the amount of time spent doing it. Once someone has done great work, it makes no sense to try and keep them at their desk, burning them out and getting diminishing returns. It ultimately comes down to smart, motivated, productive people who need to do great work. When they get it done, they're done.

These two employees are Conversio success stories. We benefited from their association with us, and they benefited in return by an increased quality of life, a life where work doesn't drain the potential for the best things. With quality of life, it's not just that a life has quality, it's that a person themself expresses quality in what they do, everywhere they go. People ripple outward, benefiting still others. Rippling out from Conversio is a benefit to society through two employees who had the space to expand their potentials.

Besides the rings of self and others, there is the final ring, that of business. In the next chapter, we'll explore life profitability in the context of business itself.

REFLECTION

*"An individual has not started living until
he can rise above the narrow confines
of his individualistic concerns to the
broader concerns of all humanity."*
—Martin Luther King Jr.

Have I truly started living? Where are my immediate interests actually holding me back from making progress toward those goals?

Where are my goals and needs in alignment with others?

Where are the overlaps between my needs and others' needs? Where can we combine our ripples, efforts, or efficiencies?

Who are those others in my life? Who can I identify by name or group (i.e., team versus a particular team member, friends versus my best friend)? Who is most affected by my actions or nonactions, by my attention or neglect? And who are the more generic others that use up my attention? Where should I change this?

CHAPTER SEVEN

LIFE-PROFITABLE VALUES

THE PRIORITY OF BUSINESS

Profit will come not from taking advantage
of one another, but from efficiencies gained
by understanding each other's problems
and meeting each other's needs.
—Yvon Chouinard, *The Responsible Company*

M ost of us believe that scarcity is the way of the world. This reductionist view reduces those who live by its bleakness.

An entrepreneur driven by the notion of omnipresent scarcity reins in risk taking and boldness in favor of defensiveness, worries that loss may be as permanent as an amputation, and sees competition as a zero-sum game that is no game, but is instead actually a war. Life and death, feast or famine, kill or be killed—such dark, pithy, easily recalled dichotomies speak to how thoroughly we have accepted the shadow of scarcity within our minds. And what lives within our minds is our doing and undoing. The scarcity mindset is a dark genie constantly whispering about the possibility of death and destruction over life and abundance.

But despite what we've been taught, scarcity is not a permanent and omnipresent force dictating the rules of our world. It's not an objective fact like gravity or mortality or time and energy. Scarcity is circumstantial. Change the circumstance and scarcity becomes moot. Solve the circumstance, solve scarcity.

Scarcity is actually just a sign of a snag, a chance to fix or improve something, perhaps with new distributions, new efficiencies, or about-time innovations. Scarcity, then, is just another opportunity in a world abundant with opportunities for us entrepreneurs to seize.

And that's what actually rules human life: abundant opportunity and, in that, the opportunity for abundance.

And not just abundance for the one but for the many. We ought not focus on finite resources—scything, hoarding, consuming, and then fretting over them—focusing on the only here and only here right now. Instead, we must seek out sustainable resources that continue to flow with happy stewardship, new resources that we discover or create, resources that we share in a reciprocal way in an ecosystem that works for and supports each member. This is a must in our life-profitable businesses; we want to make things happen in the world, not see things die. We want to make something live where nothing was before, not play undertakers in the business of subtraction. As life-profitable business owners who know that scarcity is temporary, we build structures that let life vine out riotously, ensuring that our businesses survive and thrive. When we recognize abundance as the ruling force, scarcity a mere pretender, we entrepreneurs have the chance to create businesses that are so abundant, so fruitful, so constructive that we nourish not just ourselves and our others, but the larger world itself.

As we've discussed, a pebble striking the surface of the flowing time and space that is your life creates a series of concentric circles. Your actions (and sometimes nonactions) are the pebble striking the water. So, from the center where you are, the force of the pebble creates a larger ring to the others who are most directly touched by you. From there, a new ring forms: that of your business, which touches still others, including the collective of your society. From your thoughts come the action of throwing the pebble, each action extending far from your center into the wider world.

What's rippling out from you? Is it hope or fear, limits or largesse, me or we? It's time to trade in your philosophy of scarcity for one of abundance to create a business that traffics in life profits as its driving force in the world. It's time to understand that life-profitable businesses, by creating sustainable work practices, are healthier businesses better positioned to sustain a customer base.

GROWTH AND SCARCITY

Earlier I touched on one of the unhealthy, unquestioned entrepreneurial mindsets: that of perpetual growth. Unfortunately, as Frederic Laloux points out in *Reinventing Organizations*, "We have reached a stage where we often pursue growth for growth's sake, a condition that in medical terminology would simply be called cancer."

If you buy into such toxic entrepreneurial archetypal mindsets, naturally, your business practices will follow from them. In the case of endless growth, it creates a few serious problems. First, we know that this "never enough" way of thinking has dire consequences for us entrepreneurs. It sucks us in, convinces us to never disengage, and to feed our lives and our shared lives with loved ones to the dragon.

The mindset also looks at market limits as a cue to adopt an aggressive acquisitive attitude. From a scarcity mindset, growth can only continue if it takes it from other businesses. But, as Peter Diamandis points out in *Abundance*, "When seen through the lens of technology, few resources are truly scarce; they're mainly inaccessible. Yet the threat of scarcity still dominates our worldview." It comes down to a belief that there's only *x* amount of money, customers, and so on, which means that for me to build a successful business, I need to win, and someone else or everyone else needs to lose.

But in your niche, that's probably not true. In most markets, opportunities are probably abundant enough for us to have multiple sustainable, healthy businesses that operate in those spaces. This situation challenges us to differentiate by understanding and meeting the needs of those customers we are best suited to. It challenges us to pinpoint the customers we *actually* want, those we can serve best in alignment with our values. In this we see possibilities for partnerships and growth instead of grasping reductionist policies that react to scarcity worries.

The endless growth/scarcity mindset grounds you in the measurement world, firing up the fear/excitement adrenaline-surge cycle every time you look at the numbers. This is far from the abundance and possibility mindset you need as an entrepreneur. As a functional entrepreneur, you need to take risks, try new approaches, and create opportunity and life profits. Let's start here, then, questioning the flawed notion of infinite growth to reenvision how and why we want our businesses to perform.

Especially because all things, including unhealthy practices and goals, generate outward ripples. We don't want that legacy for our businesses and for those who help us run them.

"GROWTH ENOUGH" GENERATES ABUNDANCE

Why do so many of us dream of a single million-dollar business in a market? Why not ten companies instead—each a hundred-thousand-dollar business? It is the same success in terms of dollars, after all.

The first scenario does let you the entrepreneur get to say the words, "I built a million-dollar business!" But the second scenario, when you think about it, is even more impressive. Not one success story, but ten of them, if success is measured not only in cumulative dollars but also in terms of ego gratification. Imagine saying, "Yeah, I built ten successful businesses."

What would it mean if all entrepreneurs actually attended to the second scenario, where smaller life-profitable businesses coexist in a market? If ten different businesses owned by ten different entrepreneurs coexisted in a single market, each business would have left room for other entrepreneurs while still providing for those the business touches. Ten companies means there are more central hubs generating ripples outward toward a variety of interests. This scenario provides a helpful diversity for the community and lessens the chance of overreliance on only one, which is safer for the communities they draw from for employees and commerce.

Within the businesses themselves, many different kinds of people can do well because there are ten different spaces for ten different entrepreneurs and ten different teams to do things in their own way. We're empowering each to live profitable lives by giving them the chance to arrange things in the way that's best for their own smaller teams. Whereas if a single business has to encapsulate all the employees, there's probably a notion of some kind of common denominator. It likely means diluting the uniqueness of each business and its approach to doing business. In terms of abundance, there's more opportunity to create life profitability in a business that can operate with smaller teams. Smaller teams mean more individuality, more ability and space to focus on who I am and who we are as a team.

In effect, by rejecting "infinite growth" and "growth at all costs," an entrepreneur who demands not only financial profits but life profits as well, helps distribute opportunity more evenly. If a community is the cake, an entrepreneur's business is the fruit inside, evenly and generously distributed, providing abundance and preventing scarcity. You can be part of that, refusing to play the zero-sum game. It's better for you, your team, and your community to create a company that does not define success solely based on growth.

If you've really bought into the bigger is better model of success, the notion that smaller is healthier and better in the big picture of things might seem counterintuitive. You might feel nervous rejecting the idea that you need to reach certain kinds of new revenue or profit levels or team sizes to merit whatever the gold-medal equivalent is in business.

But the blanket idea that bigger is better can, in some instances, be an outright fallacy. Mass and vast farming jumps to mind, with food traveling great distances, massive swaths of land subdued to generate profits, resources artificially diverted to service them, small farmers driven out, lack of crop diversity, cost to wildlife and climate—when we add up the costs, economies of scale are revealed as a woefully incomplete function. No matter the harvest, if you look at the larger picture in the macrocosm of the world or the microcosm of your particular world—if the costs cause harm, they are not life-profitable.

In light of that, we must ask ourselves if growing our businesses beyond a certain point is the best goal for our lives and the lives of others our business touches. What would be too much growth and why? What would be growth enough for a healthy business that produces abundance without harm?

Engaging in the Position of Strength

Instead of just continually shooting the lights out, aiming higher and higher, believing that up is competitive and all else weakness, what if we operated from a sense of strength? We all have weaknesses, and if they are damaging, of course they need to be addressed. But for many of us, weakness is just humanness. There might be some discrete amount of improvement we can make, but then we hit a wall. At that point, we can practice the wisdom of hiring someone who actually is an expert instead of trying to do it all ourselves, a common mistake on the entrepreneurial journey.

Our real opportunities relate to existing strengths. Ask yourself where you can double down on them. For entrepreneurs, one strength is an ability to explore the possibilities of what is out there. The scarcity and fear mindset might have gotten you stuck where you are because whatever you're doing right now *is* working on some level, even if it's hurting you. Maybe you're making just enough to have a passible lifestyle for your family, but no more—certainly not enough for long family vacations. Maybe you could step back a bit, but it would create a temporary disruption: a step back might turn into a setback. But again, that's a scarcity mindset. Make provisions and then open yourself up enough to explore opportunities. How might your business change how it does things? You want a business that sustains itself and sustains you. Just that.

My previous business, WooThemes, was based on the WordPress open-source content management system. That meant I was always involved in the open-source community, and the products I built initially inherited that open-source license. Bottom line: anybody could purchase any of our products and resell them because that's what the license allowed. The only thing the license required was that we at least be given credit for the code we wrote.

The consequences were twofold: open source meant there were a lot of players in our space, creating a diverse ecosystem. In the WordPress ecosystem, hundreds of companies were spinning up, eventually probably thousands, all making a great living. Yes, there were bigger companies in that ecosystem, sequoias in a forest. But that didn't deter the smaller businesses from also building healthy businesses for themselves.

The community respected the rules of the open-source game. Instead of looking at competitors as enemies, we were friendly. In fact, we at WooThemes were friends with most of our direct competitors. Yes, we were competing with each other. Yes, if we all had to pitch for the same project or a first-time sale, we went hard at that. But we never did it in a way where we jeopardized friendships. Relationships mattered; open source created greater openness in relationships, certainly a life-profitable mindset.

The second consequence of being part of an open-source community is that it forced us to really think about our strengths and double down on them. Although I'm extremely competitive, we didn't have to beat or kill our competitors. We just needed to figure out who we were and what unique value we added to the ecosystem within which we were operating and competing.

If anyone could copy our products and resell them, what could we do that they couldn't copy? What were the things that really set us apart? It came down to our branding and customer service, two things firmly rooted in our culture and values. In WooThemes' culture, actions spoke louder than words. The way we put ourselves out there in branding or marketing, our interactions with customers—such things were aligned with who we were as a business entity and who we were as individuals.

Nobody felt threatened. We weren't worrying that someone would drive us out of business or that we needed to be absolutely gung-ho in blocking competition. We weren't constantly in fight-or-flight mode, where it was only going to be the survival of the fittest, driving our employees and loved ones to stress and distraction.

Instead of rallying employees around a shared enemy, which isn't sustainable anyway, we rallied them around our shared culture and values. That's very sustainable, a positive way to keep people motivated and productive. Instead of war and scarcity, we practiced a mindset of abundance. Creativity, innovation, service, and value in the world for those our business touched—these inspired us. And it was enough to create a unique value proposition that sustained our success. It's akin to writing: everyone has the alphabet and the words to create stories. Yet there will never be a cap on the tales we can tell. In an ecosystem relying on every player contributing unique strengths, coexistence helps all. It increases abundance, this diversity of contribution. And cross-pollination ensures leaps in evolution and even more opportunity.

Working from abundance generates positive morale and supports health. Nobody should be in that mindset where every day you trudge to work to fight the competition, to beat it back or beat it down. "Beat" it: the negative vocabulary reflects unhealthy mindsets. The alternative approach is "I am going to work because I want to do great, meaningful work today, and I want to share that with the people around me for whom I care. *And* I want to work in such a way that when I leave work, I can actually take my whole self home to my family, my friends, and all the other parts of my life, as well!" Depletion shouldn't be the normal situation at work. Nourishment should be. Nourishment sustains.

SUSTAINABILITY: THE IMMEDIATE PRIMARY GOAL

To avoid a workplace of depletion, a life-profitable business looks to sustainability as strategy. We've just established how abundance is sustainability is nourishment, as far as your team is concerned. Your business is organic too, dynamic and growing and in need of nourishment. Nourishment sustains business. In other words, sustainability is the lifeblood of a business.

This is a challenging notion for those living out the entrepreneurial archetype, where the journey involves lasting as long as you can, burning through fat stores and water stores and everything else, hoping to live long enough to hit pay dirt. What a strange way to conduct business. Why not just invade Russia in winter?

It might seem impossible, but you must find a way to make business sustainable from the very start. In the early days, entrepreneurs often feel like the fight for survival leaves no room for something as comfy as sustainability. It's a hand-to-mouth enterprise for so many of us. We have to burn our fat to survive the winter, we think.

But, no, you must preserve and ration the very finite resources, including yourself. You are running a marathon. Don't risk injury in the beginning. Choosing a strategy of sustainability from the start is the safest way to ensure your fledging business survives.

Start by concerning yourself with the pragmatic, first-tier consideration of sustainability: is the market perspective or perception favorable enough that your ideal customers will actually spend enough money with you to sustain your business operations? In other words, you need to make enough money to not run out of cash.

Next, you must think about sustainability in terms of resources. If you have a jewelry business, for instance, obviously you're going to need certain amounts of precious metals and gems. Look at your own, processes in terms of sustainability. What are the inputs, ingredients, or components you need to do your thing? Can you ensure sustainability in terms of availability? Can you adjust processes or your inputs to increase your sustainability?

Then look at sustainability in terms of human beings, both individually and collectively. You've explored the life-profitable value of self. Think about it now in terms of what your sustainability requirements are as an individual. And, since we entrepreneurs are an ambitious lot, perhaps consider personal sustainability with a conservative eye. Ask yourself, *How do I prevent myself from burning out? How do I protect my own mental, emotional, physical wellness and health whilst I work on this thing? How do I do the same for others? How do I sustain my team on this journey, keeping them motivated and aligned?*

And then there's the notion of sustainability for the society and markets in which we operate. How much are they willing to accommodate and accept what you do? If you operate within a greater community (like the open-source community WooThemes belonged to, for instance), do they look favorably on what you're doing?

Sustainability can't be limited to a single aspect, so you must assign sustainability a holistic meaning.

Sustainability is a way of life, a feedback loop that keeps the machine moving forward and enables profitability—and life profitability—indefinitely.

DEFINE GOOD ENOUGH

To really have a sense of what healthy sustainability looks like for you, your others, and your business, you need to have a "good enough" measure. Without a good enough measuring stick of some sort, you're not capping excesses. You're already saying that you're prepared to enter some never-ending marathon. That's clearly not sustainable for anyone, even we entrepreneurs flush with the belief we can do anything if we just try.

I had to ask myself that question—*What's good enough?*—during a challenging time at Conversio. Conversio operated in a competitive, saturated market space. Any kind of marketing software finds itself in such a congested space. And then we got into email marketing as well, which, in some situations, is even more competitive.

Loads of our competitors made aggressive moves. Some were incredibly well funded. And they were willing to raise more money, something I didn't do because it didn't align with my particular value of independence. The market and the way everyone else played the game led me to question whether our practices were sustainable in the long term, without having to compromise our values. It wasn't that our competitors were wrong, but for my team and me, following suit would not have translated into life-profitable practices.

There was a trade-off here. Either I stuck to my values, which made business inherently sustainable for me, or I tried to fudge a little in the short term in the hope that somehow things would play out and lead me back to my proper path. In other words, the question was compromise myself or stay true.

I think everyone faces a tempting situation that argues that a short-term compromise justifies a long-term gain. I also think everyone knows that fickleness never leads to a return to constancy and fidelity.

I stayed true. Things were loosely good enough if I made some hard decisions. I had to lay off two employees, an incredibly stressful and sobering move. Shortly after that, I began challenging my business expectations in light of our landscape. If I wasn't going to change our life-profitable culture, I'd have to adjust in other ways, starting with deciding what growth revenues were acceptable if they could at least achieve a viable, successful, life-profitable business. I was on a quest for good enough.

It was part of a multi-month process for me, involving a series of decisions and actions. The first was to say, "Let's be profitable as best we can, and let's try and do that without relying on revenue growth. Let's start building a safety net in terms of cash reserves."

As soon as possible, I decided to diversify my personal financial interest, making conservative investments outside the business instead of investing my all into the company. I didn't yet know what was good enough, but I knew it didn't mean not paying myself as a stopgap measure. I'd done that for two months when I laid off the two employees. Of course, that wasn't sustainable.

Paying myself became one baseline for good enough. And while I was at it, good enough could not involve draining my personal financial interests in favor of the business. I could not indulge the business at my family's expense. Removing the possibility of an Adii bailout influenced my decision making. It also created a healthy boundary, which made me a better entrepreneur: I ran the business; it didn't run me.

Being a better entrepreneur by practicing the life-profitable value of the self will always lead to a better business. Remember that nourishing and sustaining yourself lets you lead your business from a position of strength, even in hard times. And, remembering our concentric circles, a better business gives you more chances to positively affect others and society. Searching for "good enough" ends up bringing clarity to what is actually doable, helping you make appropriate decisions and take action.

My "good enough" measure further crystalized when I initially thought about selling Conversio. We had a couple of inadequate financial offers. I started the negotiations.

Thinking through the offers gave me a bit of a framework in terms of what would be okay to accept. It came down to thoughts like *Okay, I'm happy to sell for* x; *I'm not happy, but okay, to sell for* y; *and I'm okay not to sell the business, to continue on as is, if I'm only offered* z. *If the last happened, I'm okay to keep working the business.* The last scenario revealed my good enough.

But why was it good enough for me? What was the context? The biggest consideration was realizing I was actually pretty happy with my life at that stage, regardless of what was happening in the business. The happiness in the rest of my life supported my activity in my business. I could sustain what I had to do there because I was content. I had gotten to good enough levels in the rest of my life.

Again, sustainability was important there because I essentially made a decision based on a holistic look at what was good enough—my realization that my life, aided by the life profits I'd gotten out of my business, could sustain me. I could continue doing the work as long as I had this kind of life.

Good enough felt like liberation.

If you asked me today what my good enough is, I'd have to reconsider. Good enough is something that shifts regularly, if not consistently, based on your circumstances, experiences, and needs. At different stages of my life, I would give you a different good enough definition than that of my Conversio days. Before I had kids, for example, my perspective was wildly different. For you, it may be a case of an elderly parent becoming sick, and you deciding you can't invest in your business as much as you used to. Less is good enough. Or maybe you fall out of love with the business; your new passion is a hobby that you've found. If the business has a team running it, what they can do without you could be good enough to sustain your life and the business.

For me back in the fresh post-layoff days, it was a matter of first getting things sorted: I moved to get that first level of profit and diversification and safety nets in place because those were within reach. It was literally saying, "What can I get from this thing right now to make it good enough?" I was not doing it arbitrarily, saying this business needs ten or a hundred times more before this is going to be good enough. I did it based on the practical reality of my circumstances. Good enough is not an artificial, external goal. Good enough comes from an internal sense of being fine, which itself rests on what you treasure and value, what you want and need to live out.

Values and Boundaries

There's no right or wrong in terms of what good enough is for each of us. Good enough serves as a beacon for what you want to do in business and in life. We move in the direction of good enough, and when we reach it, we note it. We don't just skip past this milestone in favor of the next shiny goal.

We stop, celebrate, and reorient, updating if need be, our answer to the "What's good enough?" question.

In the larger scheme of things, the answer(s) must involve what you value. Values include consideration of time, people, and costs. "Good enough," then, can be imposing time boundaries, choosing the kind of people we work with and the things we're willing to do. It causes us to create limits that respect the other people affected by our actions. Reaching the good enough, then, allows you to live from your real values. They set your boundaries, keeping you steady on the path to your sustainable life.

Operating according to good enough creates breathing room and space to look at your life in a larger context. Good enough reveals the characteristics of your rich life. All these values and characteristics provide a framework to think about larger issues such as legacy, contribution, how business can serve those, and how business cannot serve those. Good enough profits your larger life through such insights. It profits the whole of you.

And, of course, the whole matters. When we weigh our actions for good or bad, the whole must be part of the reckoning. Life profitability is a fiduciary responsibility between you and your life that has as an outcome sustainable, conscience-saving measures. In living out good enough, your values become omnipresent.

And they become measurement tools with which we weigh policies, decisions, and actions. Values also serve as feedback, measuring how close we come to living them out. I'm not talking in just an abstract way. These are "in real life" tools applied, as I mentioned earlier, to decisions. They can serve as an oracle. If you ask your clearly defined and relevant values, "Should I do this?" they can give you the answer and tell you why. If you can't figure out a course of action yet, values can say, "Well, you know all these other paths are off the table. What's left?" Values, in this way, make concrete boundaries.

Applying values and their attendant boundaries ensures that, as we create something of business value in the world, we also create life-serving values in the world. The more we entrepreneurs throw our pebbles into the lake, the greater the impact will be on society as a whole. In this we are entrepreneurs in a fuller sense than we tend to realize. We are life entrepreneurs, and we touch the wider world. We must start to think holistically, not just about our business scopes, but about how we impact the world.

REFLECTION

*"Abundance comes from within;
it comes from thought, intention,
attention and expectation."*

—Deepak Chopra

What is my intention with my business? What parts are getting the most of my attention? And what is my expected result from doing all of this? Are these things aligned? How does this affect life profitability? How could adjusting my intention and aligned actions increase life profitability and abundance? How can "good enough" help me increase life first?

CHAPTER EIGHT

MODELS OF LIVING PROFITABLY

BUSINESS

*We have become reactive to the competitive
landscape, rather than responsive to the needs of
our communities—those people we hope to serve.
We are so focused on the competition, or even the
threat of it, that we've forgotten to double down on
what makes us and our work unique and valuable.*

—Bernadette Jiwa, *Story Driven*

A British philosopher named Alan Watts introduced
the West to eastern philosophies and religions.
Some of the ideas he shared relate directly to us

entrepreneurs. First, that notion of the sequential journey of education, work, and then...the end, life spent up.

In that ending, a lucky few of us will have some winter years in which to try to really live while progressively getting less able to, since we're on the way to dying. Watts instructed us to instead play during our lives—play the way people play music. No one is playing or listening to music to get to the end or to get there the fastest. No, we enjoy it in the present, singing along or dancing, letting it fill our hearts. And that is how life should be, enjoyed playfully all the way through.

This mindset needs to be applied to our business. The best businesses play the game not to compete or win, but to create value and impact beyond themselves. If you enjoy your business and reap life profits for yourself and others, even if your business fails—and you, thus, lose the game—you reset the board and play again. Only next time, you are more experienced, and you've still collected life profits.

If you play in the competitive mindset of life or death, it won't be so easy to reset the board. You'll be depleted, burnt out, your ego suffering, and you'll probably have exhausted the emotional reserves of important others like family or partners. Your recuperation period will be longer than if you had been focusing more on life profits and life first than if you depleted yourself trying to get first to a finish line. Of course, failure will suck no matter how you got there. But wouldn't you rather have gotten there singing and dancing? Wouldn't that help you find the inspiration to get back into business? How much better to be eager to play the game again instead of girding up for another war.

As we've discussed, entrepreneurs traditionally tend to focus too much on competition. Everything's a fight. "I have to win a deal. I have to fight against others to win this deal. I have to beat my competition in the market." It reduces our experiences within the business and sucks the marrow from the fun of the challenge.

There are huge amounts of fulfillment and stimulation in building a business. But focusing externally on competition takes us out of ourselves and away from our core self, which is where our richest veins reside. Those are the resources we control, the resources that we can use to build a better business, a better life, and a better world. Instead of allocating resources to beat the competition, we need to allocate toward developing what is unique to us and our distinct capabilities to stand out in the market. Doing so will manifest as a unique offering. And it will feel great. You cannot feel restricted or constricted when acting in alignment with yourself. It feels like flow.

Focusing on the competition also takes us outside the orbit of people important to us, people whose worth enriches lives around them, including our own. Likewise, our communities are our collective others, and serving them through our work products and services improves not only their lives but ours. But, of course, we must do that in the context of our values, not just for financial incentive. In that way, our businesses become a higher expression of ourselves and those involved. Some of that expression is in the form of life profits. Including life profits in our understanding of success provides a fuller gauge of our business accomplishments.

WHAT BUSINESS SUCCESS ACTUALLY MEANS

When we start making life profits, the ambition of greater business aims must wait. Specifically, I urge you to resist the temptation to put EBITDA (earnings before interest, tax depreciation, and amortization—let's just simplify it to profit before tax) above a life-first approach. I understand the pressure can be enormous, as if business is life and death, but it isn't. Life and death are only truly significant when it literally comes to life and death.

Recall Maslow's hierarchy of needs, which attempts to break down what each human being needs for a full and fulfilling life, from basic survival needs to love to self-actualization. All that can only happen with life time and life space. Prioritizing EBITDA more often than not crowds out both space and time, putting it at odds with our human needs. Human needs first means EBITDA alone cannot be how you measure your business as a sustaining and successful undertaking. It's not that EBITDA is wrong—just too narrow for we who realize that we cannot separate business from life. Success is no success when it destroys our larger well-being. Success isn't success when it does not stand up to measures that expose how meager are our lives. Broadening our definition of success to something wider than the usual standard of EBITDA opens up a range of possibilities for more significant greatness and profits. The greatness ripples into the world, meeting its needs. Life profits profit the world around us, spreading abundance instead of scarcity. Let us explore, then, how we can model life profitability through our businesses.

EXPLORATION

Many younger entrepreneurs are in a rush, as I was, running fast to get in the entrepreneurial game. But success isn't limited to those on the young side. Statistics show that older entrepreneurs, even all the way into their sixties, have a higher success rate in terms of building businesses that ultimately have some significant economic value. For many of those, it's likely not their first run of the game. They've probably had at least one or two rounds before that.

The lesson here is that we don't have to squeeze everything into our twenties and thirties and forties. You're going to have more than enough time to build significant things. Then the question becomes, what is that significance?

I, of course, think the answer is to build something life-profitable. Because playing a round of a life-profitable game means that even if that round comes to an end, you've accumulated so much life profit that you can just take it into the next round. All your personal development, all of the connections you've made, whether friends, family, or community, sticks. Experience, skills, evolution, bonds— all of those things are still there.

And therein lies another lesson: survivability. The mortalities you actually need to worry about are yourself, your loved ones, and your relationships. A business can die, and you can spin up another business. Businesses are ultimately just shells. They're legal entities. They're ideas. There are thousands of ideas. There are thousands of opportunities. A business can respawn. Its ending is therefore survivable, even if painful. You can't respawn yourself. You can't get back life profits you didn't accumulate when you had the chance. So, in setting priorities about risk that you want to mitigate against, the personal ought to be higher than business.

Diversification

The best way to mitigate risk is diversification. If you're all in on this business success and that's the only thing your ego is getting its claws into, there's no diversification. That's a massive risk. If, instead, this current idea, this current business, this current team, even—if they're just one part of broader life-profitable pursuits, it minimizes everyone's risk of pain and loss and recovery time. Again, the ultimate risk involves consequences for us. Will we be able to play another round if the first one doesn't work out? Will we be able to look the people who came with us on this journey in the eyes and say, "You know what? Good game. We had fun. We tried our best. We were true. We were accountable to each other. All those good things we discussed." If you can say yes, then when you ask, "Can we play another round now?" the answer is likely to be "Yes, I'm willing to risk again."

This revives the discussion we had around the concept of "good enough." "Good enough" helps us rein in excessive expectations that don't serve our larger life. Usually, those expectations center around getting more. Recall the earlier reflection quote by Seneca: "It's not the man who has too little who is poor, but the one who hankers after more." In other words, we don't need to amass more to be wealthy. We need to amass the right things. If you've defined your good enough, you have the chance to invest in your "right things." That might, for instance, be true human connection with others, self-enrichment, or open time.

And certainly there is a component of a comfortable amount of money that allows your business to underwrite your richer life. This is a different mindset than using your life and money to underwrite your business for its enrichment. The first is life-profitable. The second is life-draining.

Because life doesn't stop during work, having more "right things" applies there, as well. You might free yourself to do more meaningful work by delegating. You might enrich your work by showing up in a different way or understanding work as an act of self-expression. You might consider whose lives you touch and focus on how to enhance them through your business. Perhaps, as we did at Conversio, you pay your vendors' invoices straight away to do your part to support their healthy cash flow. Perhaps you reduce your employees' weekly hours or start providing more vacation time or encouraging them to take lunch away from their desks. You might incorporate learning and skills development as a regular component of work, letting in more creativity and innovation.

The point is, by focusing on the "right things," you create space and life profits that can be redistributed as you would distribute dividends. Then you can diversify your life according to whatever mix of risk and investment makes sense for you.

Economies of Better

Scaling up to get unit costs to go down, thus increasing profits, is a commonplace aim. One way to gain that efficiency is to rely on work specialization. That might not be right for every employee. Some need variety in their work menu and a sense of a greater context. Without it, their engagement falls.

Other employees might be artisans who love specialization. In many companies, such experts get promoted or given extra responsibilities, changing the scope of their work. These employees are now misfits where once they fit. Their specialization had yielded economies, now reduced or lost. And the team member isn't as happy either.

When entrepreneurs gather a team for a life-profitable business, they've got to consciously understand the "right things" their people need for a rich work life and rich collaborations. A good relationship with the company and between team members leads to better results. You're looking to optimize for that. And if you do, you'll gain the economies of better that come with flow and smooth operations.

This life-profitable approach to facilitating employees' best workplace can't function well in monolithic companies. They aren't able to adapt and flow around employees and shift processes and systems to deliver the best workplace solutions for individuals or small teams. And communication and decision making are too slow as well. If you have the good fortune of building a large, financially-profitable company, at some point you'll likely be at odds with life-first practices for your employees. If you scale up still more, you might even make business less life-profitable for yourself.

But you don't have to design your company to grow to a mammoth size. You can instead purposely design it to reach that "good enough" figure, thinking about how it relates to the rest of your life, and then tweak the business over time to generate as much life profits as it can for you and your team. You may even discover a new market need that justifies a second or third "good enough" business that complements the first, diversifying your entrepreneurial portfolio. All the time, there is less life cost. This, too, is an economy of better, with more opportunities for constructive dynamics to ripple out into the world and into the future for what could be years, decades, centuries. It is a stimulus. It is the legacy you will leave that arises from values you hold and act on right now, while you're alive.

Good Enough

Being alive and present to be counted is implicit in your "good enough" measurement. In the last chapter, I explained how good enough arises from what you value. But let's explore some of the considerations that will help you arrive at that good enough minimum goal.

First, you must look at your life portfolio, all the different elements that need to work together right now. In light of that portfolio, the first criterion for good enough is doing no harm to your life right now.

Second, for good enough to be, well, good enough, what you value needs to be represented in your life right now. The logistics and coordination of what you value deserve some consideration. You might realize, for instance, that you need to spend more time with your children, but that you also need your business to keep operating at a certain profit threshold. What do you have to reshape or rework in your business for that to happen? You're supplying the ingredients to create a recipe for life.

You can imagine your good enough life of the future, a time when everything is good enough for you to feel fulfilled and content, then reverse engineer it. Add up the time, space, and finances that you need for living that life, and then start building those into your life and business right now instead of pouring 100 percent of yourself and your money into your business for the next five years, hoping it will all turn out.

I, for instance, no longer wanted a commute or the office waiting for me at the other end. As an introvert, I didn't want to necessarily see people other than my family every day. I also wanted to be on hand for my children. Since I understood what I valued in the context of my well-being, I decided on a fully remote and distributed team for Conversio. Immediately, the company profited my life instead of costing it. My ideal version of work was possible immediately, so I immediately built it in.

Some of your ideal components and practices my not be possible straight away. Begin shifting your business to get there. Incremental change works. It's manageable. The main thing is to think it through. Be as clear as possible with yourself and as specific as possible. It's not set in stone, but if you're going to start, you need a starting point.

PRACTICES

We've talked about culture as an expression of values. Values tell you what to do and what not to do. By intentionally living out values, we can intentionally create culture.

Our culture at WooThemes didn't arise that way. By the time we started thinking about culture a couple of years into the business, the culture was already there. It had arisen out of the fabric of all of our interactions and collaborations and behaviors. It wasn't a detrimental culture, but it didn't add value either.

This was a big lesson for me. Starting Conversio, I understood that culture could be a contributing factor to life profitability, so I deliberately thought about values and what we were setting out to do. Culture is the context for all actions. It can steer decisions and amplify efforts. It can also muddle decisions and efforts. I realized that culture wasn't some abstract notion but something to be purposely practiced.

After WooThemes, I wrote a bunch of notes on what I'd do differently or better next time. An important one for life profitability was, "I will build a team sooner." At WooThemes, I had been a control freak, always too slow to empower and equip someone else. In light of this, Conversio being fully remote would have important cultural implications. I wanted culture to lead and influence my team, whether I was there in body and mind or not. We'd be in far-flung places and time zones, and I didn't want to be on call, constantly tethered to work through my devices. I had a blank slate to begin building our culture, and writing out notes turned out to be the genesis of our evolving values as we matured.

Building Culture in Phases

If you are at or near the beginning of your founding, there are three phases to building culture. The first phase is looking at your personal values and seeing how they might apply to your business. The second phase involves developing the culture you want to cultivate (or recognizing what you have if your business has been around for a while). The third phase amplifies awareness so culture guides behavior and decisions.

Phase One

You've already done a lot of that thinking work as you've gone through the book. Now consider those that have an aspirational component which can serve also as purpose and motivation. What do you aspire to as an entrepreneur? What whole life do you want to live as you create the business? You can't leave life profits out of the equation.

Aspirational values also can point toward undeveloped abilities and even weaknesses. It's important to acknowledge those. As Rand Fishkin pointed out in *Lost and Founder: A Painfully Honest Field Guide to the Startup World*, "A founder's weaknesses are often baked into the company's DNA and create a figurative kind of debt." Acknowledging those figurative debts allows you to plan for your company's evolution.

It's important when you write that first version of your culture that it can't be too far away from where you are today. If I, for example, start a new business and declared that we will be the most extroverted team in the world, that's probably going to fail. I'm not the most extroverted, and I just can't jump the chasm between reality and aspiration. Be realistic about where you are at today, but build in that slight bit of aspiration to add steering and direction. Make it as specific as you can. Generalizations don't build practical scaffolding for your culture.

Phase Two

Phase two of culture building includes the nucleus you've gathered around the owner or partners: the first team members. At this phase, Conversio was about a year old and had a team of six or seven. We got together in person and started putting words to what we knew about ourselves and what we say within our own unique culture, Conversio's particular lingo. I call this phase recognizing and following symbols. It's the insider vocabulary and context born of shared experience. If you pay attention to those symbols, you'll find a beacon shining on your culture.

This unfolded for us in ridiculous ways that captured the playful camaraderie the team shared as part of our culture. For instance, Adam and Rick came from Northern Ireland, and they introduced us to three very specific words the whole team used. They're not exactly proper English. In place of nice, we at Conversio said "noice!" to give high praise. We didn't say shit; it was "shite." If you acted an idiot, you were being a "shitehawk." It might seem superficial, this shared Conversio dialect, but as a remote team it personalized us to one another, creating bonds across distances.

In this second phase, finding the natural cultural symbols that arose from shared context strengthens the connective tissue of your company's culture. To start, have everybody just begin noticing what's already there in your business. See what's naturally bubbling up in your business and note it. At Conversio, certain phrases kept coming up from my team, for instance, "cost benefit." My wife, Jeanne, likes to point out that no matter the conversation,

I can work a financial term into it, in this case "cost benefit." I had been financially transparent with the team to let them have the context of what and why and where we were. It had become part of our shared culture. The team was on the same page with me, thinking about cost benefit and using the phrase conversationally. My quirk had worked its way through Conversio culture.

By the time we'd met for two or three team retreats, our culture had become consciously codified in the symbols and language we enjoyed. We had become a practicing culture, perpetuating it through use. Culture was not merely unconscious socializations. It had become a value-driven tool by which we could examine our shared behavior and our actions, and make decisions. We'd finished phase two.

Phase Three

The third phase of building and strengthening culture is to amplify awareness. The purpose of this awareness is to make sure that culture leads and influences a team regardless of who is present in any conversation. When discussing an option for us, cultural language popped up because it was the vocabulary we shared. When we needed to go back to the drawing board, we'd start from our shared cultural values. If a decision was a toss-up, the deciding factor always came down to how to best practice our culture. Practicing culture through awareness strengthens it, and that strengthens your company. It brings your brand into focus to the outside world and gives everyone inside behavioral guides. As the leader, you must keep up the drumbeat, persistently and consistently speaking to cultural values. You must amplify awareness.

If your company isn't new, of course you'll need to start at phase two, trying to notice your existing symbols, and then go back to phase one. It's hard to quickly pull the semitruck over to a different lane if your culture has been entrenched, but you can begin to make adjustments, let them gel, and then adjust further. That begins with an investigation and conversations that try to put words to the implicit things happening in team members' interactions across all parts of the business. You'll need common understandings, the vocabulary for them, and vigilance as you begin adjustments. Decide desirable and undesirable, constructive and destructive characteristics, and start making plans on how to make shifts.

Sometimes these changes will mean changes in team members. Some people will not align with the company anymore. They deserve to be helped into a situation that better fits them. This process is actually mutually beneficial if it's done well. It's about transformation, not decimation. If Sally doesn't fit into the team anymore, we can help her find a spot somewhere else. That's a win-win, life-validating approach. And it validates your culture. Cultural fidelity means integrity.

Attracting and Hiring the Right People

Culture is an important tool in attracting and hiring the best people for your company. These are the people who benefit your company, who can, by their very presence, like Mama and Papa Bear for Conversio, add life profits for others. They are also those whom your company benefits because they share values you can support and help them express.

When your culture is understood and actively lived, it's great to publish it and your values on your websites for hiring purposes. That will help candidates decide if they want to be a part of your team. Hiring for fit is what you're after. Of course, you need the minimum skills and experience. But that's only 20 to 30 percent of the conversation. All other considerations come down to what candidates can offer as members of a community.

Because the bulk of our company's communication is written and asymmetrical, it made sense for us to ask questions demanding long-form written answers. For instance, "Why do you want to work for Conversio?" The answers let us know if they would be able to communicate effectively in our remote work conditions, but we also learned what they valued about the opportunity. It was clear some would be happy with any job. But some mentioned culture and values, saying, "I just love the idea of being family first. I'm a young mom, and I just had my second child." Those who were clear the opportunity was not just the work position but also the life-first agenda turned out to be the best hires.

After the first round of having applicants communicate through written questions and answers, the second round was a text-based Q and A. If an applicant really invested time on it, they'd probably spend about thirty-odd minutes. For the third round, we asked applicants to send a sixty-second video introducing themselves. Would they be comfortable in this format, comfortably engaged and contributing in real time?

The final round was a video-call conversation. I asked questions geared toward an applicant's alignment to us, specifically about how they grappled with failure, challenge, and learning, and about self-discipline and routine. I'd ask things such as "Where do you go to learn new things?" or "Tell me about the last big failure you had in your career," or "What does a normal day look like for you?" As a young company with remote workers, the ability to cope with failure, challenge, and learning while managing workload without direct supervision was important.

We used all these hiring measures to see if applicants were temperamentally appropriate and aligned with our values and culture, and because any future teammate would need to be comfortable communicating in the formats used during the process. They're a big part of how Conversio conducts business. Importantly, I, and later a rotating hiring committee of our most tenured members, tried to hire for mutual and reciprocal abundance. You must adapt your hiring approach to suit a life-profits and life-first mindset, taking your culture and values into account. You aren't hiring just to fill a work slot. You are bringing someone in to be part of a culture making productive ripples outward for the abundance of everyone involved.

Financial Foundations

Many entrepreneurs start without a strong understanding of cash and accounting profit and loss. No problem: you can hire a financial adviser. Doing so is a good first move, but you have to gain greater financial understanding. The responsibility for decisions is yours, and you ought to make those decisions informed. Your financial adviser can "tutor" you in this regard as you learn what you need to make informed financial decisions, decisions that rest on understanding possible consequences.

Since a lot of entrepreneurs have hazy notions of the financial end of things, they aren't necessarily apt to be consistent and constant when it comes to bookkeeping. This creates all sorts of problems and all sorts of rationalizations, which usually amount to some form of kicking it down the road: "I'll do it at tax time. I'll hire someone to sort it out. I've got it in my head, so I'll just do the bookkeeping later."

None of that is life-profitable. You're giving yourself future work, while hamstringing your present self in matters of decision and control. Life-profitable practices free room in your outer and inner life. A great life-profitable business must model financial foundational practices that safeguard the business. It may be tempting if you feel exhausted at the end of the day, the week, the month, or the quarter to just put off all the recordkeeping. But that is like throwing away a compass while trying to find your way through a forest.

Consistency is key: consistent attention and consistent recordkeeping. You want to trust your numbers. You certainly don't want to constantly go back into those numbers to investigate seeming irregularities. Have good data coming in and consistently allocate and report it in the exact same way. For instance, label your expenses and keep those labels consistent as you record them. Spend time on this so that you can trust the picture the data paints. Disorganized and incomplete recordkeeping costs you in stress, in competitive advantage, in time, and in money. Recordkeeping is important.

The only reason that got done at Conversio was because I did it. I had an advantage in my accounting degree. You can create an advantage by realizing that financial understanding is not something to defer but to take on right now. It's a language that lets you look at records and understand their tidings.

If you aren't the accountant yourself, you need to initially invest time with whoever is doing it for you to set up books for consistency. Then seek their advice on how to make your books' categories a little bit more telling. Ask what categories your adviser needs to see. These records yield data, and data yields insight if you know how to speak their language.

Financial insight allows you to make quicker, wiser decisions. There's a lot of uncertainty in entrepreneurship. This financial aspect doesn't have to be one. When you couple comprehension with attentiveness, especially over time, you'll understand what's happening. You won't have to become a sleuth when signs of a problem begin surfacing. You'll understand your business's trends, whether up or down, you'll understand the context of your most recent data and what it might mean, and you'll understand what you might need to adjust to reach your objectives.

Trends are important, showing a possible future based on past financial data points. Financials are always a lagging indicator, showing results of past actions and decisions. Thus, when you get your financial reports, check them against trends. Use differences in ratios between periods, and then ask questions about those differences. This makes your recordkeeping all the more important: the quicker you get to high-fidelity reporting, the more proactive you can be when presented with changing trends. Then you can rely on your newly gained financial vocabulary to express what you grasp intuitively or deductively with stakeholders or with those who can provide insight.

Many of us entrepreneurs at least understand the basics. But curiosity about what lies beyond your existing knowledge is crucial. Bookkeepers or accountants or tax advisers will just say, "Listen, pay this thing," and if you ask what it is, they'll answer in a nutshell. But the thing is, they are not invested like you are. Your part-time accountant is invested in his own business. You owe it to your business, your workers, your vendors, and yourself to gain at least conversational fluency in the language of financial workings. If you add this knowledge, building greater financial understanding and vocabulary, you can eventually rely less on external consultants. Taking on more of the financial end of things puts you on more intimate terms with your business, which eventually expands your decision making ability. Expansion is space, and space is life-profitable.

Though financial literacy gains you independence, you'll still make use of experts, say in regulatory or tax matters. Or to ask more advanced questions instead of basic ones to accountants who charge you in, say, fifteen-minute increments. With the clock ticking money away, you're less apt to swallow and nod as an accountant briefs you if you can get expert instead of basic advice. Financial literacy is a sort of superpower, and the more you understand, the more you can wield that power to add resilience to your business through responsive, informed action.

Shed Weight, Move More Freely

One of the added benefits of keeping on top of your books is a familiarity with expenses. When you stay on top of them, you're getting wise to the story that's playing out in your business. You can influence that story, making sure to write it the way you want to be. You can hold other involved people to that story and make them accountable. This story is one where you run a lean business, not a bloated one. It is lean by your resolve to cut unnecessary expenditures.

Often, especially in financially successful businesses, there are recurring expenses that no one understands. What are they? Why were they incurred in the first place? Sometimes they're small, so you don't stop to take them out; you just keep paying. But a little exploration in a business on top of its books usually reveals these expenses shouldn't be part of the current narrative of your business's story anymore. They're not part of the current moment, so they aren't adding to the storyline you're writing with your current cast of characters. It's time to cut.

Cutting unnecessary expenses is not a simplistic kind of goal. It's about profits. You must ask yourself, *How do I maximize my financial output for the least amount of financial input?* That's how you maximize financial profit.

If you're able to cut those unnecessary expensive expenses and be lean, it does two things. First, it allows greater agility and flexibility because you're literally not carrying excess weight. Second, it frees up space and resources. Reinvest elsewhere, or if you're at that "good enough" place in your business but not in life, make life-profitable deposits. Stop wasting space and resources on things that are not contributing to life profitability.

We typically underestimate our ability to save and cut expenses and so instead pursue profits. Unfortunately, as our business profit grows, our lifestyle costs tend to increase too. This makes us a slave to constant growth. Meanwhile, we also take on recurring expenses, such as software subscriptions. You may be underutilizing them. Some businesses may not be using them at all. Can you do without them? In the story of your business right now, do you really need them?

Some people spend money on perks that seem to have a benefit, say, catered lunches for a small team. Sure, it's free for your team and they may appreciate that, but it keeps them tethered to their work instead of spending their lunch time in their life.

And maybe you thought having an office location was right. Is it still right? Actually, was it ever right or do you have an office because that's the "way it's done"? Have you asked your employees if they'd rather work remotely? It saves commute costs for everyone and eliminates a substantial business expense.

Shedding the weight can be upsetting because it takes us out of the status quo, which can make us feel insecure.

You may feel a sense of ambivalence and even grief as you leave some old ways behind. You're charting your own course now, though, not following the path of others. And freeing space and resources gives you the chance to deliberately reinvest and redistribute for new, better growth.

Constant Diversification: Reinvest, Redistribute

Acknowledging that diversification minimizes risks, how can you, the entrepreneur, apply the practice to your business? Well, first you must remember that we're not talking about your business in a vacuum. We're talking about your business as a subset of your larger life. If your business makes money, conventional wisdom says to reinvest it to make still more money by growing a bigger business. But remember, you're challenging conventional wisdom now. Your business shouldn't become an enormous fire-breathing dragon torching the rest of your life.

Instead, diversify by, for instance, building a better home for your family, a home that nourishes a better family life. What would that better family life look like? How can that home investment support it? How much business profit should be redistributed and leveraged toward life profits to create a richer life while investing in a real estate asset? Consider saving some of the money your business generates and putting it into other asset classes so that if some kind of economic event hurts your business, you have other financial levers to pull. It might seem counterintuitive not to go all in on your business when you're on a winning streak—or at least not a losing streak—but you certainly won't reinvest and redistribute when you no longer can. Do it when times are easier than they could be if and when your business faces a crisis. During one particularly good year at Conversio, we found ourselves flush, and I faced a decision about where the money could go. I thought over the choices with return on investment in mind. First, I could diversify my personal financial interests, weighing that against reinvesting in the business. Or I could save it, creating financial room for a rainy day, gaining increased security and peace of mind. I could redistribute it to the team to strengthen their own situations. I could also make a charitable contribution to community organizations, thus having the impact of our activities ripple outward. In the end, I distributed the money to the team: "We had a good year. Here's some extra money." Besides building that connective tissue between all of us, redistributing to the team meant many ripples flowing out as each employee made decisions about their extra money as well.

Don't stop at reinvesting and redistributing money. Do the same with your time, your energy, and your attention. Pull some of those from your business and reinvest in your important relationships and personal development. Doing so will probably call on you to redistribute work-load to your team, which means giving up control a bit.

But your business, since you've put in the work to build a proper team, can benefit by having everyone invested so that no one disproportionately carries it. Diversify responsibility to mitigate risk—and to free yourself up for the rest of your life. Investing in others and your own personal development builds strength to call upon when business—or life—becomes more difficult.

Constant diversification means having your "good enough" measure of business success and your understanding of what wealth is to you front of mind. Remember that wealth acquisition is not about having more but having the right things. What is life-enriching to you? The answers are the life portfolio you're building. You redistribute business profits there, turning business profits into life profits.

Review Your Allocations

Just as you would with a financial portfolio, review your time, energy, attention, and financial investments in your life portfolio according to some weekly or monthly cadence. Review to make decisions on where to invest more, where to divest, and where to switch your attention, vigilance, and tactics to get the results you want for your life portfolio.

Besides that regular review, you'll need to ask for feedback. My business coach has weekly meetings with his wife to look at their life portfolio, but on a monthly basis, they review each other. So the question might be literally, "Hey, Jane, give me a rating about me as a husband or how I've been as a dad." The feedback gives needed information about how current investments in time, energy, attention, and money are performing. The information lets you make corrective adjustments.

I've talked about energy, time, and attention; all those need space. It's understandable that when you achieve efficiencies and do free up space, you naturally want to plow those profits into the business. Of course, we're all hyper-ambitious, right? But you are not just a business entrepreneur; you're becoming a great entrepreneur of your life. The question is, then, should the freed space go toward more work or toward more life profits?

EXPRESSIONS OF LIFE-PROFITABLE BUSINESS

Once your business has reached the "good enough" threshold, giving free space to employees or self won't compromise the business. So the consideration here is, having reached the "good enough" threshold in your business, have you likewise reached the "good enough" threshold in your life? If not, of course life wins over business. If you have reached "good enough" in both business and life, probably you can feed freed-up space and resources to both the business and life profits. The point is, actually

202 ◊ LIFE PROFITABILITY

make a conscious decision that expresses your values and life profitability.

Elasticity

Elasticity is an expression of a life-profitable business. Rigidity in life speaks to an attempt at mechanization and control instead of allowing life to express and adapt itself in whatever way furthers growth and self-fulfillment. To facilitate life, businesses have to be elastic, able to adapt and absorb the new across time and circumstances. This isn't to say there is no structure or unifying ideas. It's to say that your notions of how the business should be run are more like strong opinions, but loosely held.

Elasticity is a healthy trait, for it injects your company with the nimbleness needed to react quickly to market and industry conditions. There are many unforeseen circumstances an entrepreneur must navigate, hidden reefs and sudden storms that often require new ideas and approaches if the business is to find a way forward. Elasticity—that ability to bend around yet snap back to an original shape, ready again to bend around the next challenge—lets a business reshape itself without breaking, even during terrible storms.

Besides bending without breaking, another quality of elasticity is the ability to take on diverse shapes. You can take advantage of that shape-shifting aspect by diversifying for various futures. We know to do this with our financial portfolios. So, too, should we consider diversification for future business eventualities, knowing we'll need to reform our businesses to suit different circumstances. For instance, we know that once per decade or so, there will be an economic downturn. In 2020, the coronavirus pandemic caused that downturn. If, before the downturn, you hadn't been doubling down on investing in your business, but had rather diversified by saving and investing in other places alongside the business, you'd have been in a healthier place to navigate the thornier circumstances the downturn brought.

Businesses already used to reshaping to and absorbing circumstances will have the means and experience to adapt more quickly to a new reality than others. For instance, pre-virus, a number of businesses and industries could have experimented with remote workers, either partially or completely. Those slower to react to the virus's imposition of distancing had not yet explored the opportunity. They had to scramble in a patchwork way. Problems surfaced quickly. Some didn't know how to support employees new to work-from-home situations. Some of them "didn't get it," expecting workers to clock in at the same times despite the fact of children being home—children who needed remote schooling or homeschooling from parents. Such companies didn't possess the elasticity necessary to support a diverse set of circumstances and reform around the challenges.

Worker diversity also supports the elasticity of life-profitable businesses. The mix of skills, personalities, and experiences all aligned with company values causes employees to behave as a sort of A-team that can pull from their very diversity range for new ideas, processes, and approaches to meet the challenge of the times.

And those workers individually tend to be more elastic than colleagues forced to live within strict roles. Life-profitable businesses have made room for them to sing and dance with life, to recall Alan Watt's advice. They have more practice meeting life on its own terms, filling their days with what's in their best interest as circumstances evolve and unfold. When something unexpected happens, workers' self-investment serves as a buoy and can help provide orientation. They know how to flow into new times and find their place within it. They don't need as much acclimation time as employees used to living in narrow roles controlled by others.

It stands to reason: if you are clear on your values and have built core habits to support those values, new circumstances call for adjustments, not a wholesale reinvention. When the pandemic struck, many people had no idea what to do with themselves during lockdown. They fell into a sort of pocket limbo outside "normal" life, rather than living out hobbies and habits already in place.

Distributed Work Changes Things

We've discussed a remote work structure as a way to promote life profitability: workers have flexibility and more room in their lives, and the resources that went into office costs, for instance, are recaptured. Of course, not every business can make the transition. If your company can, though, making the move to distributed work will change not only your operations but the way the team relates. For one thing, remote work has a chilling effect on the tendency to micromanage.

Many traditional businesses have a notion of "bums in seats": if I can see you in your seat, then I know your computer's on. It doesn't matter what you're doing, but you seem productive. And I can hover and jump in anytime.

Obviously, you can't do that when you have remote workers. Instead, you're essentially building a structure that is individually led. Each is on their own journey, working from wherever they want, however they want, in ways totally aligned with who they are. They cooperate with their teammates, their fellow journeyers, and they gain genuine trust with one another by their dealings.

This trust is different than in traditional workplaces, where there can be a sense that someone above them directs them to cooperate by giving them roles to play. In remote teams, independent individuals voluntarily choose to become accountable to one another and the company.

And you must express trust in your people as well. The notion that if you aren't there to monitor them, workers will devolve into laziness insults workers' integrity and abilities. It also reflects poorly on your hiring practices and your methods of setting expectations and modeling vision and values. Remember that during the interview process, you've made sure that there is significant alignment and overlap of values and characteristics. That gives new hires a sense of the familiar, ushers them into the team, and promotes smoother communications.

Letting go of micromanaging and extending trust has a great effect on team members. Their sense of freedom—not license—lets them ease into their own appropriate rhythms, which in turn boosts productivity at work and happiness in general. They're not worrying about being judged by what they do and how they do it. No one is watching. If I'm working remotely, it doesn't occur to me to wonder what my manager will think if I leave in midafternoon to pick up my kid from school. It's not even a consideration.

Of course, my life and work have overlap—I have to be at meetings; I need to structure things to be available to other team members. But besides that, I can work when it's best for me, when I can be the most productive. I create my daily routines and habits in the way that provides optimal life. The business has given me life profits.

Not every business can move to a remote work model, but for those that do, the structure leads to expressions of trust, responsibility, and team rapport. It lets workers show up as their best selves, which naturally lets them give their best effort.

Openness through Transparent Communication

A remote team requires you to deliberately set up communication methods and customs that suit your particular business. But all life-profitable businesses should do the same. The goal is transparency. Transparent communication creates life profits because it avoids conditions that create stress and friction in favor of natural flow. Opaque, need-to-know, and disjointed communication, on the other hand, breeds distrust because people become unsure of what is happening.

You'll remember that at Conversio, our conversations, unless they pertained to a specific work problem or something confidential, were done as a group, sometimes in person, most times through shared digital communications. We relied on Slack for real-time or short communications, allowing us to make quicker decisions. We employed video discussions too, usually for meetings that had an agenda. We used Basecamp, meanwhile, for longform, asynchronous written discussions. Both Slack and Basecamp let us document conversations, and they're searchable, letting us look at them later in light of values, for instance. Basecamp especially gave us the means to have a legacy record of discussions that called on contributors to consider what they wanted to bring to a conversation.

By all this, we created an elastic communication structure that itself was trusted—it worked to connect us. No confusion, no unintended misunderstandings, no censure. People relied on it: it was part of the Conversio virtual workplace, a place where openness was normalcy.

Openness is room to speak and to be heard. Openness is an expression of a life-profitable business that happens because of transparency.

Controlled Growth: Slowing Down, Zooming Out

Some time ago, I read the book *Shoe Dog* by Nike founder Phil Knight. In it, he depicts the long struggle of the early Nike days when he imported shoes from Japan. It was a year-after-year struggle to navigate all the things necessary to get just one annual shipment. This was in the last half of the twentieth century—Knight started his business in the sixties—and there was no easy and miraculous communication and distribution then. One had to do, well, the footwork.

He put in the work, as we all do, but the circumstances of the day meant he had to take it slow. Year after year he struggled to get the shipments, raise the capital, sell enough. The timeline to build a business was necessarily long, and this long, slow road served as a sort of apprenticeship in building a good business. Despite slow goings,

Knight's perspective was a longer lens. He zoomed out where most of us today zoom in, looking for instant gratification. Knight's timeline was a lifetime, whereas many entrepreneurs today seem to consult stopwatches.

We have the connectivity and the processing power to spurt forward, to do things quicker, quicker, quicker. But that fuels the notion that we're supposed to be growing at exponential rates. Consider this, though: no matter how fast certain worldly things move, we ourselves must still live at a speed hospitable for human life. We have always been surrounded by things that move faster than we do— light, electricity, atomic activity—but never before have we felt compelled to match that speed. Yes, we can board the train, the plane, the motorboat, the sports car, and go faster. But we should not confuse the utility of speed, which provides time savings, with the pace at which we or our businesses should perform. Employing our modern advantages opens space for us. It is breathing room, not a whip.

Nike's breathing room was time, time to figure out what did and didn't work. We should use the breathing room that our modern advantages afford us in the same way, carefully and deliberately getting our footing and picking wise steps. If, at some point, you suddenly have a breakout success, you'll know how to avoid missteps since you've been walking the terrain for a long time and are at home there.

More importantly, if you don't slow down—if you don't control growth, it will control you. If you don't slow down, you cannot properly steer.

Patagonia presents another illustration of controlled growth. They do that by not living in the measurement world, but in the world of values. In an interview with *Business Insider*, former CEO Rose Marcario said,

> *There's no way I should make one decision based on quarterly results. I think that the whole system is built around metrics and a process that is not healthy for people and the planet...People recognize Patagonia as a company that's going to keep asking deep questions about our supply chain, the impact we're having in the world, and looking at business through a more holistic lens other than profit. Profit is important...But profit isn't the only measure of success.*

Your values are intrinsic to your understanding of true success. You control living from those core values more than anything else. These values will help you control growth through uncompromised decision making. In holding to your value strengths, you can spare your company the pitfalls of scaling up before having a truly firm foundation. We only have x amount to give, and we can't give more than that. When you give of those limited resources, you compromise on something else. Know where you should not compromise, no matter the lure of growth.

Some of the values that guide Patagonia's growth without compromise include "Cause no unnecessary harm" and "Use business to protect nature." Expressing fidelity to these values has not stunted its growth. In fact, the company has thrived even while rippling its impact outward toward dynamic environmental activism. Its financial success is redistributed in a life-profitable manner as it funds grants to grassroots environmental groups, contributing 1 percent of its annual sales. The company zooms out, looking to long-term sustainability for the business and the earth.

Meanwhile, Patagonia's notoriously loyal employees value the fact that Patagonia values them—as whole human beings with interests and children and lives. In an interview with *Forbes*, Dean Carter, Patagonia's CHRO, shares that Patagonia found that engagement went up and productivity stayed the same when the company gave employees three-day weekends every other week. Meanwhile, employees reported that they were able to improve their quality of life in areas such as relationships and community engagement.

Patagonia proves that it is possible to build a life-profitable and financially profitable business simultaneously by being kinder and more holistic, and asking our people to show up as their best selves. In conducting business, think bigger than profit and loss; go beyond that to impact. Let your values ripple outward into the lives of those your business touches and into the wider world.

In the next chapter, we'll begin evaluating where you can find the most opportunity to do this—to change your life from business-centered to life-centered.

REFLECTION

"No matter what your mission is, have some notion in your head. Forget the model, whether it's government or nonprofit or profit. Ask yourself the more important question: Is my mission improving the world? Are you sure about it? Seek to disconfirm that all the time. And if you can, change your mission."

—Jeff Bezos

The richest you can ever be is when you are clear about your mission and pursuing it. What is your mission? How does your business serve it?

How are you using the profits of your labor? Are you reinvesting that into your mission? Are you diversifying your interests?

Crucially, when has business been tough? What has your safety net been? Is your safety net wider, bigger, more elastic? Have you diversified enough that, in the toughest times, it doesn't all come down to you—that it doesn't mean you jettison your life as ballast?

CHAPTER NINE

ASSESSING WHAT'S LANGUISHING IN YOUR LIFE

Part of every misery is, so to speak, the
misery's shadow or reflection: the fact that
you don't merely suffer but have to keep on
thinking about the fact that you suffer.

—C. S. Lewis

R eading this far, you've likely come up with a couple
ideas you can put into action right now, ideas that
might seem to loosen the stranglehold your business has on your life. Action would feel so good—first,

because that's so natural to us entrepreneurs, but also because it would feel like you're moving into a solution. But no action can be a solution unless it takes you in the right direction. For that, you have to know where you ought to go, and that means starting with your right here and right now. Whether you find yourself on a plateau or in a valley without a clear path to your own summit or apex of your life, the next step is to stand still. Don't fall into the trap of taking action right now to build a sense of artificial momentum. To speed up, you will first need to slow down, come to a stop, and consult the map of yourself. You need to get your bearings; you need to get the lay of the land within.

You've already been mapping yourself as you've reflected throughout the book. I've given you a lot of life profitability language, vocabulary that must be part of any conversation about creating a life-profitable business. Values, meaning, sustainability, self-expression, abundance—such words are part of the new way you look at your business, test it, and measure it against what it costs in life. The good news: by understanding your values, those things that give your life meaning, you have your destination. Then your life gains a true sense of direction. Remember, it starts with the self and ripples out. By orienting on yourself, you find your orientation.

REVIEW YOUR REFLECTIONS

Start now by looking back over your reflections. It might be helpful to read through them for each chapter in order to rediscover the discoveries you've made on your journey so far. You might want to reconsider some of what you find back there in light of what you know now. After all, you looked at things with different eyes back then. You need the eyes of yourself right now, as you are in this moment, equipped with your new insights, to really take stock of right here and right now. As Eckhart Tolle said, "You see and judge the present through the eyes of the past and get a totally distorted view of it." That won't do. If you find that you want to reconsider any of the reflection prompts, adding to them or even repeating the reflection altogether, do so.

Pay particular attention to Chapters 1, 4, and 6, reflecting on your thoughts more than once. You may have an entirely different attitude now about what is an "entrepreneur." And examining how you have so far been modeling (or failing to model) life profitability as a function of self and of others can be revelatory.

In reviewing what you have sacrificed or compromised in favor of business, including others, you are looking at your current life's landscape. You likely see missing pieces, places where life has withered away. Though this examination may be painful, it's important to look at it squarely and without judgment. To prepare to resurrect your life, you need talk to its ghosts.

To some of you, reviewing your reflections might give rise to a sense of being overwhelmed, even triggering that feeling of burnout caused by the tug-of-war you've been living between your business and the rest of your life. That's why it's so important to stop for a moment instead of quickly going forward. You're in a safe space right now, looking at the causes of the things that pain you. And part of that safe space is to do nothing except look around. You don't have to take action until you know the right action.

Don't narrow your focus to bits of what I have said or what you have written that sparked some resolution or inspiration or an urge toward doing something—anything—to avoid what you're feeling right now. You'll end up back where you started, going in circles. If you're feeling overwhelmed and out of space, I don't want you to find yourself back here again sometime in your future. I want you to stay here, not project yourself into your own future. Give yourself a little more time before you follow your natural entrepreneurial impulses to take the next steps. We'll get to them in due time.

In this chapter and the next, we're going to go through this safe spot right here, this place where you're just looking and getting oriented before you move on to the actual doings, moving from the theory of a life-profitable business to actually starting to make one.

DETACHMENT:
AN ANTIDOTE TO RESISTANCE

Detachment comes in handy when you start to examine what's been ill-nourished up to now. Therefore, instead of leaning into your life assessment, you need to step back. You don't need to be invested in the past or the future because you're straddling them right now. You're going to look around at the current state of things based on your past actions, noticing what you'd like to leave behind and bring forward.

For now, detach enough to begin seeing where there is fallow ground or barren deserts or the need to row back to shore where you can enjoy the benefits of the business without forgetting you're meant to live on land. Detach from putting a requirement on yourself to look at your actual requirements. Pressure moves you away from detachment. Remember, you don't have to figure it all out right now. Stay at the start of this. Step back from the shadow of the business and keep reminding yourself that you and the business are not equal. You are separate from your business, and larger.

YOUR ASSESSMENT WORKSHEETS

Writing things down brings clarity of thought and account-ability to ourselves. Use the worksheets found at the chapter's end (or here: *lifeprofitability.com/worksheets*) to begin assessing where you are today and where you plan to go. The worksheets aren't something "to get right." They're always going to be rough drafts. You'll revisit these drafts often as you implement incremental life adjustments and live their results.

Even as you start assessing and plotting possible course corrections, it will be hard to resist taking immediate action on something, if only to feel a sense of momentum. If and when you do eventually give in, at least make it a small action. You aren't supposed to make a U-turn, just a few degrees of a course correction—three, ten, twenty degrees in a different direction than you are going right now.

Your life assessment will give you an idea of possible directions. Remember, though, your destination arises from your sense of meaning and values. Right now, you're just trying to find your way. By taking things slow, you won't waste a lot of time backtracking.

It's most important that you do not do the same things you did before. Make sure your "new thing" isn't just the same pattern in a new circumstance. You'll stay on the hamster wheel that way, feeling like a failure because you haven't been able to break through to new patterns. You need new and different insights and understandings to identify the right approach to your destination. Take your time with these worksheets to think, to be with yourself, to accept you actually want to make a life change here or there, to accept that you must put business in its place so your life can take place.

That's going to feel scary and stressful and frustrating and risky and sad as you think of what's gone before. But it's also going to feel hopeful and exciting and profound and, most of all, deep-down right.

Remember, if it feels like a lot, step back to detach. And remember: incremental. Since it is an incremental process, moving toward a life-profitable business step-by-step usually means that changes will only feel marginally different over time. And that's good. You are becoming an entrepreneur of yourself and this novel product called a full and rich life. There's a learning curve. Faster or bigger or bolder changes can wait until you are well entrenched, when the life-first lifestyle feels like normalcy. At that point, it will feel so natural, you'll just set the context and let life unfold.

The Life Profitability Appraisal Worksheet

Your Life Profitability Appraisal will help you take inventory of the parts of your life that are going fine, going very well, or in need of attention. The last are those things underrepresented in your life. Comparing your finished appraisal to your values will let you get the scope of the undernourished aspects of your life. Discovering that you've let friends go by the wayside, as I did after college, or, as I did, that you've resorted to managing your children for efficiencies to keep up with business demands, when family is your highest value—discovering such misalignments means openings, opportunities to enrich yourself through life-profitable business practices. Using the Life Profitability Appraisal worksheet, you'll be plotting out the characteristics of your life as it is right now and where your life profits (or lack thereof) are being spent. You're giving yourself a quantifiable starting point to use as a pulse-checking mechanism over time. From here, you're going to start taking actions and moving toward taking greater responsibility for a greater life.

You'll find both a blank and an example Life Profitability Appraisal worksheet. Studying its left column, you'll find the familiar three rings that ripple outward into time and space: Self, Others, and Business. Below those, you'll see an additional heading: Future. Notice beneath these labels are notes, such as the one with Future, which is self-actualization. Looking over these notes, you'll find they correlate with Maslow's hierarchy of needs. This is to remind you to ground your thoughts against your real human needs and how they are or are not expressing themselves or being met in the world.

The top row of the worksheet contains the labels of three columns. Each invites you to assess to what degree your needs (left-most column) are being filled through distribution of time, attention, energy, and/or money from your business to your life. You're going to do a rough estimate of where you are at the column-row intersections.

In the example worksheet, which is based on a difficult time at Conversio, find the checkmark where the Core Competence column intersects with the Accretive Habits row in the grid. (The practice of practicing a habit increasingly wires that habit into your brain, strengthening and reinforcing it into a strong neural pathway. At that point, habit is automatic. Much easier to say accretive habits as shorthand for this process and outcome.) Such checkmarks in the Core Competence column means that you've formed life-profitable practices. You're good there, and probably can't get much more, if any, improvement without diminishing returns.

Meanwhile, a checkmark sits at the intersection of Monitor and the Others ring category's Friends row. You're doing all right here, but with more attention and investment, you could improve. The question is, how much do your values call for you to invest more to see improvement? Are the places checked off good enough for right now? Or are they so important that it's time to take them up to the next level? You'll begin weighing and considering this as you do the next worksheet, the Life Portfolio Assessment. The final column sees a deficit in well-being, a signal that life profits diverted here could make a big impact.

When you check a circle in the Needs Attention column, don't assume you *should* get to work on one or more of these deficits. To shift something from the Needs Attention column to Monitor might take a redistribution that you simply don't have available now. For instance, if in my example, Community had landed in Needs Attention, budging the checkmark into the next column might compromise the time, attention, and energy needed to attend to Mental/Physical/Emotional Well-Being. Clearly, it's most important to attend to the ring of self before rippling out into community. You can't do everything at once, after all. Remember: incremental change.

Besides featuring our three dimensions of life profitability—self, others, and business—the left-hand column of the Life Profitability Appraisal worksheet has a Future element that lets you specifically examine the extent of your self-actualization. Under Future, the Continued Sacrifice row lets you assess how much you're sacrificing to your business at the cost of self-actualization. Meanwhile, Progress toward Longer-Term Goals calls for thinking about which life areas you're working toward. Are you working only toward business goals or is there a balance between business and life goals? Are you investing in longer-term life goals at all?

As you complete this inventory, a lot of thoughts and impressions might tumble over one another in your mind, say, reasons behind your circumstances or sudden ideas on how to make a shift. You may want to capture some of these in brief. But don't get carried away. This is neither a brainstorming nor exploration phase. Jot a note to stop thoughts and feelings from distracting you from the purpose of this exercise. Double down on detachment, looking at the black and white of what you're doing. You're just making an inventory.

I want you to review the sample worksheet again, with the understanding that it represents a real-world challenging time for me and Conversio. I was under pressure, feeling constricted in terms of space and freedom, and I felt stuck.

I'd already invested in some life profits then, building accretive habits, including running, meditating, reading, and some social things I'd added to my weekly routines. Family was strong, my team was good and healthy, and I had no issues with commercial stakeholders. In the ring of business, controlled growth was fine. We'd run into challenges, but it wasn't because we'd let the business beast off the chain. It wasn't a case of running two hundred miles per hour for growth at all costs. We were fine enough.

But at that stage, as you can see from the sample worksheet, our safety margin was under threat. Diversification for both the business and my personal financial situation also needed attention.

My mental and emotional well-being was likewise not fantastic. I was under immense and constant stress. The ego beast was chasing me, telling me I couldn't fail publicly. I struggled with that idea. But I couldn't convince myself that all of those nice goals I'd set myself and the hopes I had for the business were worth pursuing if I had to endure continuing stress. And because of business pressures, I felt isolated.

Looking at my future, I had realized that, in terms of self-actualization, there were some sacrifices I was no longer willing to make in pursuit of long-term business goals. In terms of life profitability, they were a life expense. I'd decided I didn't want to afford it anymore and maybe I couldn't afford it anymore. It fell into the Monitor column because I was awake to it. I had to monitor this area before making further decisions. And I had to monitor to make sure the sacrifices didn't become so burdensome that they'd plunge into Needs Attention. In that scenario, I would have needed to rethink my life and probably would have considered whether I needed to get out of the business altogether.

In terms of the longer-term goals, I accepted they'd take sacrifice but was ready to set boundaries for them in light of values that took precedence, especially family. I understood it had to be done because I was not in a great spot. In this, I'd come to a place where I was ready to shift things to put life at the center. I could slow down to shift energy to my life from the business, which meant goals would take longer. I could adjust the scope of my goals to make them more manageable.

The takeaway was that what I was doing in terms of efforts toward the future could continue, but a few things needed to change. As I experimented with and monitored adjustments toward that end, I'd find the right balance to move these areas into the Core Competence column.

The Life Portfolio Assessment Worksheet

The Life Portfolio Assessment worksheet will help you assess your circumstances as they relate to life profitability. You'll be inventorying your existing values, assets, space, and goals to start figuring out where you have room to make changes, where such changes should be made, and what resources you can bring to bear to accomplish them.

As before, you'll find both a blank worksheet and an example (again, based on my experiences). A third worksheet lists questions for you to consider as you fill out your blank Life Portfolio Assessment.

This time, the worksheet is laid out in a two-by-two grid. At the top left you have Values—naturally. Values are at the core of your considerations, your North Star. There are a few ways you can begin to figure out the most important values to list. If you'd like, consult the assessment worksheet that has questions contained in the grid. Answering the example questions will help get you started. Also, in Chapter 4, Models of Living Profitably: The Self, I told you about the thirteen questions posed in Dr. John Demartini's *The Values Factor.* Answering the questions made me think deeply about what I valued. I'm sure it was the same for you. Later in Chapter 4, you examined your values in that chapter's Reflection. Review that too.

The list will reflect your current personal values, those you want to see lived out in real life. The example worksheet reflects that for me. I needed, at that stage, to concentrate on the ring of self. For instance, I wrote "Not serving two gods/being present." I was over a year into my mindfulness journey, and I'd learned that there were many things that would detract from my ability to be present, mostly around trying to do two things at once. So, at that stage, trying do one thing at a time was—still is—an important value for me.

Assets heads up the upper right-hand square, followed by the question "What do I have to assist me in this journey?" The question is theoretical at this stage. You're not trying to make a decision about what you're *definitely* going to need. You're just identifying the things you definitely have that *could* be valuable. You can't know what you actually need because you don't yet know the direction you're traveling.

You'll be listing your strengths under Assets, the supports you can rely on as you create change. Generally, you've accumulated these strengths on your journey so far. They'll brace you when you start to feel anxious as you veer off the path you've been previously traveling. These assets are familiar, reliable, sturdy, and can inject a sense of the familiar when you venture into less familiar terrain.

And they can center you. For instance, I wrote "Business with real revenue and acquisition interest." We had offers for the business. Not fantastic offers, but at least I knew that real people were willing to pay real money for it. Looking at it from the perspective of worst-case scenario, "worst case" was actually okay—an asset. It gave me options, which you'll find in my Values column.

Moving to the lower left-hand side, you'll see Space/ Elasticity/Margin. This list uncovers where you have wiggle room to create more or reclaim space. If you're overloaded, could you make any changes? In the sample worksheet, there are possibilities: reduce business expenditures, bring in experts, bring ego expectations in line with "good enough." Assets lists strong family and friend bonds; they would support me, I wrote, if I had to work more until I created more space.

There's an interplay between Assets and the wiggle-room category that creates opportunities, with Values as the starting and ending points of your journey. But how to get there?

The Goals/Desires category provides possible directions. What do you want out of your life and business journey? How do you want to play, sing, and dance through your life, as Alan Watts would encourage?

Your goals and desires will reflect your hope ("Build a business that returns value to shareholders.") and your daily pain ("I'm not willing to be this stressed all the time anymore."). Looking over your list, how does your gut react to your goals and desires? Does your heart pull you toward one in particular? Does your intuition divine waters there that would slake a longtime thirst? Trust yourself. You're going to make small changes on the goal or desire that calls you the most or that would most relieve a burden. And you're only going to take small, survivable, "take back" risks. Their outcomes will teach you.

Refer back to your values and your initial appraisal. Couple those with your desires and goals to start imagining possible first steps toward a fulfilled and fulfilling life. Begin devising plans that could move you toward your goals and desires. Look over the assets and prioritize those that create the space for change. Let the interplay of your lists prepare you for what could come when you take action. Let your filled Life Profitability Appraisal and Life Portfolio Assessment worksheets excite you: by looking at what has been neglected and why, you find your starting point for the life you want and deserve, the life you can begin living bit by bit right now.

You'll learn how to launch it in the next chapter by choosing three concrete goals and the beginnings of a ninety-day plan. You've got more worksheets to complete and a lifestyle and business style to embark on. Abundance and freedom start now.

REFLECTION

*"To arrive at a contradiction is to confess
an error in one's thinking; to maintain a
contradiction is to abdicate one's mind and
to evict oneself from the realm of reality."*

—Ayn Rand

Without (subjective) baggage, how would you
proceed next? What are the things you truly
value? If you had a completely blank canvas,
what would you paint?

What is the legacy that you would like to
leave behind?

LIFE PROFITABILITY APPRAISAL

	CORE COMPETENCE Already creating life profitability. Unlikely to be able to improve now.	MONITOR These are likely sometimes (not all) life-profitable and could be better with more investment or effort.	NEEDS ATTENTION Biggest detractors of life profitability. Currently removing most space, freedom, or energy.
SELF Physiological and Safety Needs			
Value Alignment	○	○	○
Space / Freedom / Energy	○	○	○
Accretive Habits	○	○	○
Well-Being Mental / Physical / Emotional	○	○	○
OTHERS Love / Belonging / Connection / Empathy			
Family	○	○	○
Friends	○	○	○
Team	○	○	○
Community	○	○	○
Commercial Stakeholders Suppliers / Customers / Shareholders	○	○	○
BUSINESS Esteem / Recognition / Strength / Capabilities			
Controlled Growth	○	○	○
Safety Margin / Elasticity	○	○	○
Diversification	○	○	○
FUTURE Self-Actualization			
Continued Sacrifices	○	○	○
Goals Progress toward Longer Term	○	○	○
Creating My Legacy	○	○	○

LIFE PROFITABILITY APPRAISAL

		CORE COMPETENCE — Already creating life profitability. Unlikely to be able to improve now.	MONITOR — These are likely sometimes (not all) life-profitable and could be better with more investment or effort.	NEEDS ATTENTION — Biggest detractors of life profitability. Currently removing most space, freedom, or energy.
SELF (Physiological and Safety Needs)	Value Alignment	⊗		
	Space / Freedom / Energy		⊗	
	Accretive Habits	⊗		
	Well-Being (Mental / Physical / Emotional)			⊗
OTHERS (Love / Belonging / Connection / Empathy)	Family	⊗		
	Friends		⊗	
	Team	⊗		
	Community			⊗
	Commercial Stakeholders (Suppliers / Customers / Shareholders)	⊗		
BUSINESS (Esteem / Recognition / Strength / Capabilities)	Controlled Growth		⊗	
	Safety Margin / Elasticity			⊗
	Diversification			⊗
FUTURE (Self-Actualization)	Continued Sacrifices		⊗	
	Goals (Progress toward Longer Term)		⊗	
	Creating My Legacy			⊗

LIFE PORTFOLIO ASSESSMENT

VALUES
What are my current personal values?

ASSETS
What do I have to assist me in this journey?

SPACE / ELASTICITY / MARGIN
Where do I have more wiggle room?

GOALS / DESIRES
What are the things to which I aspire?

LIFE PORTFOLIO ASSESSMENT

VALUES
What are my current personal values?

- How do you feel about your personal space?
- How do you spend your time?
- How do you spend your energy? (And where do you feel energized?)
- How do you spend your money?
- Where do you have the most order and organization?
- Where are you most reliable, disciplined, and focused?
- What do you visualize and realize?
- What do you think about, and what is your most dominant thought? (How do I want to live my life?)
- What is your internal dialogue? (Intention)
- What do you talk about in social settings? (What makes me an extrovert?)
- What inspires you?
- What are your most consistent long-term goals?
- What do you learn or read about most?

ASSETS
What do I have to assist me in this journey?

- Reputation / personal brand
- Network (those that may be able to help out)
- Financial means
- Audience (those more likely to purchase from you)
- Team (collective and individuals / trust)
- Experience / skills / ideas
- Friends / family / life (Support?)
- Personal practices / habits

SPACE / ELASTICITY / MARGIN
Where do I have more wiggle room?

- Spouse that can cover you?
- Unnecessary expenditure that you can cut?
- Tweak in logistics to save a little more time?
- Senior team members to whom you can delegate more?
- Increased prices of product / services to increase margin?
- Additional hire (more money) that creates more space / attention for other things?
- Slowing down growth rate?
- Could you tweak your business to evolve into a peripheral space?

GOALS / DESIRES
What are the things to which I aspire?

- What sacrifices are you making today that you'd like to cut?
- What would you like your legacy to be?
- If this were the only business you ever built, what would the business look like in ten years' time?

LIFE PORTFOLIO ASSESSMENT

VALUES
What are my current personal values?

- Family first
- My home is a safe place
- Continuous personal development and learning
- Minimalism / less is more
- Curiosity
- Being uniquely me (rebellion)
- Freedom and flexibility (having options)
- Not serving two gods / being present
- Making new mistakes

ASSETS
What do I have to assist me in this journey?

- Strong family and home life (people who care more about me than the business)
- Healthy habits: exercise, meditation, reading
- Business with real revenue and acquisition interest
- Safe financial nest egg (even in worst case, we won't lose our home)
- Deep relationships with my best friends
- Strong industry reputation and skills (I could get another job)

SPACE / ELASTICITY / MARGIN
Where do I have more wiggle room to create more space?

- Reduce business expenditure / move to profitability
- Delay or change planned lifestyle expenses
- If I need to work a little more, my family would support me
- Find experts that can assist with tactical
- Tweak my ego-expectation of what the business should be

GOALS / DESIRES
What are the things to which I aspire?

- Build a business that returns value to shareholders
- I'm not willing to be this stressed all the time anymore

CHAPTER TEN

INCREASING YOUR LIFE PROFITABILITY QUOTIENT

We will learn that though we think big,
we must act and live small in order
to accomplish what we seek.

—Ryan Holiday, *Ego Is the Enemy*

I f your business has been a fire-breathing beast with endless hunger, burning you out and causing strife between you and your life, Ryan Holiday's words are a comfort. No matter how tired you feel and how big the task ahead seems, the key to taming your business doesn't lie in Herculean efforts. You only need to do the small, right things every day that steadily move you in the right direction. You can manage that. And it's sustainable.

In fact, what you've been doing thus far has been the Herculean effort. It has become arduous and odious, and it's no wonder you're in crisis, looking for a way to sustain the business while sustaining your life. Exhortations from the entrepreneurial archetype playbook—dream big, work hardest; no sacrifice is too great; you can sleep when you're dead—these don't help you. By now you've realized that living out such clichés is not a failure on your part, but a flawed approach toward the entrepreneurial journey.

It's time to reject the way society and the mainstream media tell you to run your business. It's time to refuse to put your life second to business. Your business *can* profit your life if you practice life profitability. In this chapter, you'll learn to identify what needs to change in order to open up space to do just that.

MAKING SPACE

Anyone who has gone on a trip with children or has been on a family trip as a child knows that the schedule needs to have flexibility and elasticity built in. The quickest way to be late and have a stressful journey is to plan to run your trip with the second-by-second agenda of a NASA launch. When you travel with children, you're apt to have to stop to, say, clean up the results of motion sickness. Children will plead for bathroom stops, sometimes just after you've gotten back on the road. Likewise, they will groan with hunger, as if their last meal was yesterday. Traveling with children means accepting real life in real time and making space in your schedule to accommodate it. Traveling with children cannot be a mechanized exercise in efficiency. Your day can't be a mechanized exercise either. You've got to have space for yourself. Creating it is the way to liberation. Time, energy, and a mind with room to focus are needed to begin making changes. In fact, increasing your life profitability will always involve making room. Sometimes you'll only need to create a little room. If you, say, cook a thirty-minute meal every night instead of an elaborate meal (assuming they're equally enjoyable), you're going to create time every day for yourself to read or meditate or exercise or play with your children.

Incorporating other life pursuits will need more room. Barack Obama secluded himself on a beach in Bali for a couple of weeks—a mere six weeks after getting married—to finish the manuscript of his book *Dreams from My Father: A Story of Race and Inheritance*. Obviously, Obama's exploration of identity was important enough for him to clear out all else to express his experiences and share his journey.

What's truly important to you? Become aware of the things you prioritize despite being time-starved. These may be things you actually can't fully enjoy because you can't help thinking that you "should" be doing something else. Or maybe you only spend time on what's truly important in your mind, habitually longing to read or travel or spend time with friends. If you double down on the things that are important to you, spending more time on them, you'll likely find that some less important things just drop off your radar immediately.

The next step is to just do less of everything—less work, fewer social commitments, less exercise—less.

This is a bit of an experiment, and it will probably feel somewhat artificial. But once you create that extra space by just doing less, one of two things is going to happen: you're either just going to have more space and time or you're going to experience a sort of boomerang effect as the truly most important things demand your time and attention. They might even create a rebound effect, coming back stronger.

Just doing less of everything everywhere, forcing yourself to try, even if it doesn't necessarily create space, will reveal a lot, since you'll become more conscious of where you're spending yourself across your life and business. It makes you practice moderation, and that alone can start to balance and center you. In doing this practice, you have an opportunity to experiment with what may bring you into better alignment with yourself. You have the opportunity to ask yourself about some of your expenditures: *Why am I doing this at all?*

Creating space by redistributing it is an exercise in compromise and fair trade according to value evaluation. In effect, you're re-budgeting, spending less or nothing on some things and more on others. The same goes with where you spend your attention, emotions, and physical energy. But you can also create space with better life practices. Releasing sources of stress frees up energy. More sleep, better food, exercise, and mindfulness let you do more and do it better. If you sacrificed such things to your business, it's time to take them back. They sustain you—and your business.

To make the changes you're about to implement, you'll need to focus on space in your day-to-day life. You can't take two weeks in Bali, most likely, but you don't need to. A bit of elbow room will let you make consistent incremental adjustments that add up over time.

WORKSHEETS

While the Life Profitability Appraisal worksheet inventories how life-profitable are the dimensions of self, others, and business, the Life Profitability Tracker worksheet found at the chapter's end (or here: *lifeprofitability.com/ worksheets*) gives you a way to measure your performance. The Life Profitability Appraisal points to your current life-profitable practices, in the process identifying opportunities for improvement. The Life Profitability Tracker yields performance feedback through a quotient. The feedback quotient isn't a judgment on you; it's a data point. You're mapping your life profitability journey so you can make sure you're still traveling in the right direction. The quotient is a tool that helps you adapt to your sailing conditions and trim the sails, whether you're moving upwind or have the wind behind you. Each time you fill it out, you have a coordinate. Adding new coordinates tracks your life profitability journey.

The Life Profitability Tracker

Filling out the Life Profitability Tracker is like a minimalist journaling exercise that crystalizes what's happening in your life. Like the initial appraisal, it emphasizes the three rings of self, others, and business—the arenas where your actions create ripples—and the future your ripples will create if you don't change anything. At the top of the worksheet are the measurement criteria of lagging, which counts for –2; neutral, which scores a 0; and leading, which awards you 2 points.

To score your performance in the areas of self, others, and business according to life profitability, you'll need to reflect as you might in a diary (though you don't have to write anything). What's been going on? What's been happening at work that is taking or giving to the rest of your life? Where is life profit spending lagging behind in your life? Where is it leading? Where do you seem to be standing still?

Think also about the best and worst things happening in a particular realm. For instance, in the realm of others, where do you feel the most connection right now (the best thing happening)? Where are you feeling the biggest drain of energy? If, over time, you find, say, that time with your sibling drains you, flag it as something to adjust or even to use as the basis for a ninety-day goal.

Keep in mind that we're not trying to measure lifestyle stability as a whole. We're trying to measure progress, evolution, change, flow, momentum. You're on a journey, and the worksheet records your adventures, for better or for worse. It's a way to help keep you mindful of what is happening as you travel forward.

We leave a lot of things unquestioned and unconsidered in the hustle of our lives. I want you to start noticing the accumulations of your life. It's your baggage. What's in it? If you look inside, you have the chance to unpack and jettison some things and intentionally stock others to improve your journey going forward. Your intentionality here sets the tone for what is to come.

Score yourself in each row, adding your scores for each ring area. In the sample worksheet, Future totaled 1 after Continued Sacrifices scored –1, and Progress toward Longer-Term Goals and Creating My Legacy both scored 1: –1 + 1 + 1 = 1. After you've figured out a score for Self,

Others, Business, and Future, average them. In my example, Self, Others, Business, and Future gave me 1 + 5 + –3 + 1 = 4. Divide 4 by 4—the number of categories—and you get a quotient of 1.00. What if the next time I scored myself I had made great strides in my business concerns, moving my score from –3 to a 0? I'd have a 7. Divide that by 4 and my quotient would become 1.75. And if I went from 0 to 1 in the business category? I'd end up with a quotient of 2.00, clearly heading in the right direction.

You'll want to regularly calculate your quotient since you want to keep it front of mind—am I or am I not making progress on life first? The quotient yields feedback on your performance. As such, in the beginning, you should calculate your quotient weekly. As you start to get a sense of your performance—patterns and trends, for instance— you can move to a monthly cadence.

The quotient provides crucial data for your next worksheet, the 90-Day Profitability Planner. If you successfully carry out your plan, the quotient will move. And studying your past assessments informs decisions about future quarterly goals.

The 90-Day Profitability Planner

After you've filled out your Life Profitability Tracker week-over-week, you'll have a new understanding about what's behind your life profitability quotient. That will give you the insights you need to make goals and take action. The first step is to create a plan. The 90-Day Profitability Planner one-page worksheet, also at the end of this chapter (or here: *lifeprofitability.com/worksheets*), lets you capture three goals and the basic steps toward achieving them.

But the 90-Day Profitability Planner worksheet isn't just an objective reporting on what needs doing and how. It also lets you ground your actions in a life-profitable mindset. The plan is actually a way to help you become a successful entrepreneur of your own life, involving your business in the endeavor. The worksheet taps into your entrepreneurial experience and talent in service of becoming life-profitable.

The exercise will feel familiar: you define goals and start breaking them down into concrete next steps, list expected outcomes, resources, and so on. But added to that are the life-profitable elements that ground your plan in a life-first mindset. Adding in a value alignment consideration provides a holistic perspective to what you're doing, why you're doing it, and how.

Three Goals in Ninety Days

Start with goals: key to the ninety-day plan is an iterative, incremental approach to taking action. So, every ninety days you pick three goals to execute. The key here is the time window. Ninety days is just enough time to actually plan without having to make massive assumptions beyond one quarter. And it's a short enough window that your goals can stay top of mind.

Your commitment pressures you to follow through, and when you do, it feels like you're actually making progress. Whenever you check something off within that ninety-day window, it feels good. Whereas, if you set yourself a goal that's going to take five years to achieve, it's easier to lose momentum somewhere during that journey.

When you start deciding on your three goals for ninety days, you'll have already collected granular data about what is happening in your life, thanks to your weekly quotient calculations. The granularity helps you catch issues you might not even be aware of. The bigger things that boost you up or bum you out are easy to notice, but ongoing problems you've been enduring for a while (that draining sibling) are not so visible. Looking at the data in the context of your values and the resources you'll need, the assets you have at your disposal, and the room you have to make potential changes will help you weigh how actionable potential goals are.

You're going to consult your Life Portfolio Assessment worksheet as well. Looking back at mine, you can see that the goals and desires I listed there became more focused and specific for my ninety-day plan. "Build a business that returns value to shareholders" in the Life Portfolio Assessment worksheet gets specific in my plan as the entry "Achieve monthly profitability." That goal is not only specific, it is measurable, achievable, time-bound, and relevant. You can see how I planned to turn my ninety-day goal into reality in the Action Items list.

When I took stock, I also knew I wanted a profitable, steady business that wasn't so dependent on my efforts. I put it in my Goals/Desires section, and that could have shown up in more specific terms in my ninety-day plan. I wished to give my team more ownership, which would free space for me, not just in terms of time, but in terms of attention I could apply somewhere else—maybe something that could enhance my well-being and health. I could have passed off some financial analysis tasks, for instance—but I didn't have someone on the team for that. Putting someone on it would have meant allocating resources toward it when I could achieve other goals more easily.

Remember to limit your goals to small, incremental, and iterative steps, always reminding yourself that life profitability underpins everything. That context in a limited, imaginable timeframe tends to promote goals that create space or are relatively easy to pull off without costing much. Ask yourself, *What are the three things I can do in the next ninety days that will have the most impact?*

The rest of the 90-Day Profitability Planner worksheet supports executing your three chosen goals, starting with values.

Value Alignment

The worksheet's Value Alignment section lists the values your goals express. For instance, my goal of "Be present during our summer holiday" expresses my family-first core value as well as the importance of not serving two gods in order to be present.

The values recorded can actually create a boundary in terms of how I pursue a goal. One of my goals was to achieve monthly profitability. My "family comes first" value will restrain that goal. I wouldn't, for instance, extend my work time to achieve it.

Assets

The Assets section of the plan links back to the Life Portfolio Assessment worksheet you completed in the last chapter. Look at the assets there that can assist you in achieving the goals you'll work toward over the next ninety days. You've already got these assets in your life, and now you're going to put them to work. In my case, because I had a "tenured team who understood me and the business," I could align my team to achieve my goal of monthly profitability.

Needs

Of course, it's unlikely that you're always going to have absolutely everything on hand to pursue your goals. What assets don't you have? Identify those gaps and either find a way around them or acknowledge that, by not having those things, you might need to change the tactical plan a bit.

Expected Outcome

Your expected outcomes harken back to your quotient assessment: if I achieve my goals, how do I expect my quotient to change, and how am I actually going to measure it? Predefining how you will measure the impact of completing your goals lets you assess whether what you're doing during the quarter is, indeed, bringing you closer to the life profitability change you want.

Don't give this the short shrift. It's easy to rationalize most things after the fact. Your expected outcomes hold you to your commitment and keep your actions from creeping away from your established goals. An easy way to give yourself clear expectations is through the familiar SMART goal criteria: Specific Measures let you take Actions that are Relevant during your ninety-day Timeframe.

For me, achieving monthly profitability would affect my quotient in two business areas— safety margin/elasticity and diversification. On my 90-Day Profitability Planner worksheet, the expected outcomes that should be realized are SMART: in ninety days, I'd support elasticity by increasing the monthly net profit margin by at least 10 percent, and I'd increase cash reserves to cover two months' expenses. Meanwhile, I'd diversify, repaying a personal loan and reinvesting the loan into passive instruments.

Knowing your expected outcomes lets you make a more focused action plan to achieve your ninety-day goals. And that can be a game changer, the difference between a strong or lackluster performance. You stand a better chance of increasing your life profitability quotient when there's no vagueness around how and what you're doing to achieve a higher quotient. Expected outcomes let you know what your goals mean and look like in real life.

Action Items

The previous worksheet sections have made you an expert in your goals. It's time to list your action plan for the next ninety days. Actions still only need to be high level; you don't need to include every single step. Listed actions should serve as an overview with enough details to guide you and your team toward hitting your goals.

In my action items, I would work toward increasing monthly profits by, among other things, reducing existing expenditures without compromising revenue. This includes analyzing existing expenses and considering layoffs, a painful exercise, but necessary.

ITERATIVE CYCLES: A NEW LIFESTYLE RHYTHM

You've realized by now that obviously you'll be using the 90-Day Profitability Planner worksheet every ninety days, which means you'll be filling out all the other worksheets regularly too. It's a lifestyle change. The more you cycle through the worksheets, the more front of mind they'll be, and you'll begin thinking and doing things with the worksheets in mind. You'll assess categories in your life with regard to how much you've invested life profits, you'll take stock of yourself and your life to get a snapshot of where you are, you'll look for places that give you wiggle room, and you'll do this against the backdrop of your current values.

It's a case reminiscent of diets and dieting. Some people make temporary changes to what they eat by going on a diet. Success is lost when the diet ends and people gain back their weight. Those who make a lifestyle change focus on diet instead of dieting. They learn how to eat. They consciously make eating decisions. They realize it's okay to indulge sometimes, as long as the lifestyle remains at the center and the indulgence is an exception, a divergence from normal.

The Rhythm of Revisiting Worksheets

The seasons of your life bring new challenges and new hopes and desires. Your present-day circumstances and priorities may change drastically over the next five years. The birth of a child, the discovery of a vocation, industry-changing technology—such events will likely cause you to reenvision your definition of a successful, fulfilled life.

Even ninety days can revamp your agenda. A month, a week, a day—the changing weather of your life requires you to adjust and adapt to keep yourself and actions in line with what you value right now. You can't put off setting aside time to go through the worksheet process. You need to do it regularly and habitually so that even small issues catch your attention early. You don't want to backslide into the business first, life second mindset. It's better if you can consciously respond to signals telling you to tweak something rather than being jostled out of your sleepwalking to find a problem made overgrown and thorny through neglect.

If the facts of your life or business situation change wildly in, say, six months, you probably should repeat the Life Profitability Appraisal and take stock again. Otherwise, do the assessment annually, referring to it every ninety days to revise the 90-Day Plan. It's important to consistently check in with yourself, questioning and testing how you're practicing life profitability.

And again, find your quotient on a weekly or monthly basis, looking for the trend line in pursuit of a greater life. The quotient seeps into all parts of your life, like keeping that awareness up and tracking and recording your journey. You're leaving a trail for yourself with those quotient assessments.

Whenever you sit down to take stock of where you are and the effects of your efforts, you're training yourself to be on the lookout for life profitability and the causes of what you see. You can observe the measures you put in place and analyze their outcomes: How are these things that I'm putting in place unfolding? What does it actually mean? Beyond that, having your mind focused on a single thing, which here is life profitability, will always be a positive contributing factor toward actually achieving that thing.

Since pursuing life profitability is a lifestyle pursued incrementally, you're not going to go from x to y on the scale of life profitability overnight, so you need to track it according to a cadence. You need to keep connecting to your self-awareness so it illuminates the data you collect. You can watch yourself realize yourself.

EVALUATION PHASE

After carrying out a ninety-day campaign, of course you'll need to evaluate how it went. The evaluation sets the stage for the next ninety-day cycle. The analysis is most importantly about learning and gaining insight.

If things haven't worked out the way you hoped, it doesn't mean you have failed. Perhaps your commitment wasn't where it should have been. Did something happen during the quarter that interfered? Was it a case of backsliding into old patterns because you didn't keep life profits front of mind? How can you solve for that during the next cycle?

Maybe the changes you tried to implement were a misfit for you or your team. Over the years, I have experimented with many new habits or processes that didn't stick. Experimentation is, after all, trial and error. It doesn't mean your goals were flawed. Learn something about what is and isn't suited to you and your team and make new action choices.

Evaluating less-than-desirable outcomes provides answers that prevent you from giving up on the process. You've only given it ninety days, and learned lessons make those days a gain. The lessons set you up for future success. Choose tactics that excite you more, that have a sense of promise about them. Your commitment will increase still more.

If you do achieve your goals and realize your expected outcomes, the evaluation period keeps you grounded in the present. Your non-life-profitable tendency of the past has probably been to jump into the next cycle without taking time to really nail down why your plan worked well. Find your success ingredients. They're going to end up in your Assets during the next go-round.

Another tendency is to charge forward without actually rewarding yourself with the life profits you generated.

Your new practice is to be life first right now, so strengthen that habit by experiencing the space, freedom, abundance, and well-being you've gained by your own efforts. If you struggle in your evaluation, understand that self-assessment goes hand in hand with self-awareness. The more self-awareness you bring to doing assessments, the more fruit your evaluation will bear. So, in keeping with life first right now, bring a mindful consciousness to your days. Be wise to your own ways. Know thyself. When it comes time to evaluate your efforts, much of what and how and why things unfolded as they did will be self-evident.

Move on now to once again filling out the worksheets that will set up your next ninety-day plan. As you repeat this cycle through this year, next year, the next five years, you'll see your life profits swell and your life grow in abundance, well-being, self-expression, and fulfillment. At first, the changes will hit close to home, but eventually, the ripples that you make from your incremental shift will wash out into the greater world at large.

Small actions consciously performed add up to big gains in the world. The people you touch, touch others; the community you touch, touches many others. Probably you aren't solving giant issues like finding a cure for cancer or coming up with a way to land the first people on Mars—those take a giant investment. But I would argue that the collective efforts accrued from ripples washing out in all directions across time add up to momentous effect that shifts the movements in the world, albeit quietly.

Do make space every day to do the small things that put you at the center of your life, living it out as your most authentic self. The incremental changes you make from a place of your core needs and values create ever-expanding life profits. Even a one-degree change in course will eventually take you far from the unhappy, unwholesome, and costly entrepreneurial path you've been traveling.

The ripples you create by generating business life profits will nourish you and others, and those ripples will keep traveling, even after you're gone.

REFLECTION

"It is not the man who has too little who is poor, but the one who hankers after more."

—Seneca

You reflected on this quote after reading chapter 1. How have your answers to the questions changed? What is your new idea of a successful entrepreneur? How will turning a life profit in your business change your feelings about it and the place it has in your life? As the entrepreneur of your own life, how will pursuing *yourself* make your life richer? How will you touch others?

LIFE PROFITABILITY TRACKER

	Lagging -2	-1	Neutral 0	1	Leading 2	
SELF — Physiological and Safety Needs						
Value Alignment	○	○	○	○	○	
Space / Freedom / Energy	○	○	○	○	○	
Accretive Habits	○	○	○	○	○	
Well-Being — Mental / Physical / Emotional	○	○	○	○	○	Total Self ☐
OTHERS — Love / Belonging / Connection / Empathy						
Family	○	○	○	○	○	
Friends	○	○	○	○	○	
Team	○	○	○	○	○	
Community	○	○	○	○	○	
Commercial Stakeholders — Suppliers / Customers / Shareholders	○	○	○	○	○	Total Others ☐
BUSINESS — Esteem / Recognition / Strength / Capabilities						
Controlled Growth	○	○	○	○	○	
Safety Margin / Elasticity	○	○	○	○	○	
Diversification	○	○	○	○	○	Total Business ☐
FUTURE — Self-Actualization						
Continued Sacrifices	○	○	○	○	○	
Goals — Progress toward Longer Term	○	○	○	○	○	
Creating My Legacy	○	○	○	○	○	Total Future ☐

TOTAL LIFE PROFITABILITY QUOTIENT ☐

LIFE PROFITABILITY TRACKER

		Lagging -2	-1	Neutral 0	1	Leading 2	Total
SELF Physiological and Safety Needs	Value Alignment					⊗	
	Space / Freedom / Energy		⊗				
	Accretive Habits					⊗	
	Well-Being (Mental / Physical / Emotional)		⊗				**Total Self: 1**
OTHERS Love / Belonging / Connection / Empathy	Family					⊗	
	Friends				⊗		
	Team				⊗		
	Community				⊗		
	Commercial Stakeholders (Suppliers / Customers / Shareholders)			⊗			**Total Others: 5**
BUSINESS Esteem / Recognition / Strength / Capabilities	Controlled Growth			⊗			
	Safety Margin / Elasticity		⊗				
	Diversification	⊗					**Total Business: -3**
FUTURE Self-Actualization	Continued Sacrifices		⊗				
	Goals (Progress toward Longer Term)				⊗		
	Creating My Legacy				⊗		**Total Future: 1**

TOTAL LIFE PROFITABILITY QUOTIENT: 1

90-DAY PROFITABILITY PLANNER

THREE GOALS FOR THE NEXT NINETY DAYS

ASSETS

NEEDS

VALUE ALIGNMENT

EXPECTED OUTCOMES

ACTION ITEMS

90-DAY PROFITABILITY PLANNER

THREE GOALS FOR THE NEXT NINETY DAYS

- Pick three goals that you believe you can successfully achieve in the next ninety days.
- Goals can be focused on creating space, pursuing low-hanging fruit, or achieving highest impact.

ASSETS

- Which of the assets that you already have will likely be helpful here?
- Is there anything / anyone on which you need to lean to create greater space to execute?

VALUE ALIGNMENT

- For each goal you set yourself, what is the most important value you need to be aware of?
- This can either be a proactive focus or definition of "no-go" zones / boundaries.

NEEDS

- Is there anything that you know now that you will need but don't have?

ACTION ITEMS

- List in greater detail the actions you need to take to pursue each goal.
- This should be a high-level tactical overview which you'll use to inform the project plan.

EXPECTED OUTCOMES

- Based on the quotient questionnaire, which realms of life profitability do you hope to impact?
- Define how you will measure your success for each.

90-DAY PROFITABILITY PLANNER

THREE GOALS FOR THE NEXT NINETY DAYS

- Achieve monthly profitability
- Be present during our summer holiday
- Create something else

ASSETS

- Need my team's alignment on goals
- Small team and our agility to make quick, proactive decisions
- Jeanne's support and understanding
- My knowledge of finance and accounting
- Being majority shareholder / ability to execute on decision

VALUE ALIGNMENT

- Family first
- Freedom and flexibility (have options)
- Don't serve two gods / be present

NEEDS

- Full assessment of expenditure
- Revised revenue forecast based on lower growth targets

ACTION ITEMS

1. Reduce existing expenditure without compromising revenue
   - Analysis of existing expenses
   - Consider layoffs?
   - Ask for discounts from providers
   - Prioritise tech debt that reduces infrastructure cost
   - Investigate changes to team retreat

2. Revised growth strategy
   - Updated product roadmap
   - Calculate ROI per marketing channel
   - Reduce/delay/eliminate underperforming channels

3. Forecast expected profitability
   - Cadence of personal loan repayments?
   - Team incentives

EXPECTED OUTCOMES

1. Mental / physical / emotional well-being
   - How do I feel when I go to work?
   - Am I excited?
   - Am I regularly sleeping eight hours a night?

2. Safety margin / elasticity
   - Increasing monthly net profit margins (target 10%-plus)
   - Increasing cash reserves (target two months expenses)

3. Diversification
   - Repayment of personal loan
   - Reinvestment of loan in passive instruments

CONCLUSION

*My life had been building potential, potential
that would now go unrealized. I had planned
to do so much, and I had come so close.*

—Paul Kalanithi, *When Breath Becomes Air*

*There are things that children grow up into.
Things like feeling part of a family, belonging
to a religion, thinking that reading books
is important, loving animals. Cady will
grow up into the idea of visiting a grave.*

—Lucy Kalanithi, widow of Paul Kalanithi,
"My Funny, Feisty, Thoughtful,
Brave Girl," *Meditative Story* podcast

Despite his many amazing accomplishments, Paul Kalanithi did not finish building the legacy he thought he'd leave behind. Nor did he expect that one of the legacies he gave to his daughter would be instilling in her an understanding of death and, therefore, of life. That legacy rippled forward, living on after his death.

He "had planned to do so much," but it's important to embrace life as a thing to live first, right now—not later, at a time you may never see. Of course, the stakes in business are high, but after all you've learned and reflected upon, you know they're even higher for you: life and death. We must make sure that our entrepreneurial journey is one that enables life and promotes it—a whole life, a life lived to its fullest. To do that, we must build life-profitable businesses.

Moving business from the center stage of our lives and putting ourselves at life's center gives us the best chance of fulfillment. From that core, we can create meaning for ourselves and others by living as an expression of our highest values. Whatever we do ripples out, after all, moving through time and space into the lives of others and the world forever. In a sense, actions even ripple backward into the past, reforming narratives about lives that have gone before.

We all want our very lives to be a legacy of meaningful action. But you have to commit to and take action on that—on opening up your own universe of possibility. You understand now how to model life profitability from that position of greatest strength: you. It all starts there.

And though we start and end this life as individuals, the ripples we create wash out, for better or for worse. We must make sure that this legacy of ourselves is purposeful and right, expressing our self-actualized self. And we must make our business facilitate that development.

What does meaningful legacy mean for you? I've asked you to reflect on this before, and I'd like you to continue to do so. The entrepreneurial journey you traveled before reading this book might've meant a legacy of absence because you have largely been absent in life, missing in action, missing in your actions, missing because of a work-first mindset. Before, you felt you had no choice about that. It's the way things are "supposed" to be done.

Now you know better. You have the tools, the vocabulary, and the awareness to adjust your journey, not only as an entrepreneur of business but as an entrepreneur of your life, thereby changing your legacy.

When I think about legacy, I think about my boys and the difference that living life first and now means to them. And what it means to me.

It means really showing up every single day, manifesting more of myself so that they see and experience that. I think of it as leaving a path of breadcrumbs for them to follow to get home to the heart of me, even if I am long gone. I think about breadcrumbs they'll find in the anecdotes they'll hear from others I touched, whether through the life profits I shared with my team and community, or the life profits I paid myself to spend time with my best friends and my family. I want to show up in all of those spaces as often as I can to make sure the breadcrumbs are there.

I want the same for the people who love you. Decide right now that instead of costing your life, your business will profit it. Make that commitment to use those profits to show up as your truest self, pursuing those things you value most as often as you can. Make your life real, vibrant, and whole, and in turn help make the lives of others likewise richer.

If I ask you to tell me about the life you want to live, it's a way of asking you to answer the greatest existential question of all: What is the meaning of life? It's different for each of us. It's even different across the legs of your own journey as you change and evolve incrementally over time.

It's a confounding question with profound answers. But life reveals it when it is an expression of a life lived true and well.

Start finding your answers by embarking on your new life-profitable life. Finish your ninety-day plan. Commit to it. Embrace it. Embrace yourself. Start achieving your first set of ninety-day goals right now.

Welcome to a renewed life.

ABOUT THE AUTHOR

Adii Pienaar is a life-first entrepreneur who writes.

While not a great fan of labels, he strives to achieve and make his own: family man/dad, entrepreneur, and writer. He also values learning and regards himself a seeker. Today that mostly manifests itself in the way that he tries to craft his life and business with his highest value in mind: family. Doing so has been a journey of self-discovery, making mistakes and reconnecting with the artist within. Less science, more art.

Adii is a self-defined impulsive writer who always writes for himself first: writing has been one of his best, therapeutic tools over the years. He shares his writing in an effort to seek connection and hopes that someone learns or realizes something that could contribute to their own journey. He also writes as a way to leave a legacy and breadcrumbs for those that want to learn more about him.

In the past, he has published three books. *Rockstar Business* and *Branding* are available for free download from his website. His first collection of poetry, *Motion*, is available on Amazon. *Motion* is a somatic journey dedicated to poems about the challenge of creating something of value and putting oneself out there without selling out or losing oneself.

Adii's current commercial gig is his new startup, Cogsy, which was first unveiled in October 2020.

Previously, Adii founded Conversio in 2014, where he tried to do things a little differently. It is also through his experience in building Conversio that he stumbled onto the idea of creating a business that could be life- and family-first. Conversio was acquired by Campaign Monitor in August 2019 and subsequently rebranded to CM Commerce.

Before Conversio, he co-founded WooThemes and WooCommerce way back in 2007, when he was still going by the name "Adii Rockstar." Before, in between, and alongside Conversio and Woo, he has worked on many other projects/ideas/startups that just didn't work out.

Made in the USA
Middletown, DE
16 November 2021